Ganja Millionaire

Kenwa Jabuki

H420 Media

H420 Media also publishes its books in a variety of electronic formats. Some content that appears in print may not be available in electronic books and the converse is also true.

Library of Congress Control Number: 2012934094

Jabuki, Kenwa

  Ganja Millionaire: Opportunities in the Hemp and Medical Marijuana Industries / Kenwa Jabuki

ISBN 978-0-615605-685 (Black & White interior)

1. Cannabis 2. Marijuana 3. Entrepreneurs 4. Business

Printed in the United States of America

10 9 8 7 6 5 4 3 2 1

And I will rise up for them a plant of renown, and they shall be no more consumed with hunger in the land, neither bear the shame of the heathen any more.
—Ezekiel 34:29

Marijuana in the Headlines

* Medical Marijuana is now a $1.7 billion market rivaling the annual revenue generated by Viagra - MSNBC (2011)

* Global Commission of Former Presidents Say Legalize Marijuana - CBS News (2011)

* First House of Hemp Made In UK 2010 - The Telegraph (UK) (2009)

* California Doctors Say Legalize Marijuana - LA Times (2011)

* Indiana State Panel of Experts Say Marijuana Prohibition Has Failed - Indiana Business Journal (2011)

* Marijuana May Be Studied For Post-Traumatic Stress Disorder (PTSD) - Washington Post (2011)

* Mayors Nation's Mayors Call For New Drug Policy - West Coast Leaf (2011)

* National Black Police Association Endorses Marijuana Legalization - NY Post (2010)

* Calif. NAACP Endorses Legalizing Marijuana - CNN (2010)

* Marijuana Ingredients May Fight Bacteria - Science Daily (2008)

* Nation's First Ever Marijuana Tax - ABC 7 News (2009)

* Why Pot Could Be State's (CA) New Cash Crop - CNBC (2010)

* Legislators Aim to Snuff Out Penalties For Pot Use - Drudge Retort (2008)

* U.S. to Yield Marijuana Jurisdiction to States - SF Gate (2009)

* Obama Administration Will Not Seek Arrests for People Following State Marijuana Laws - Fox News (2009)

* Marijuana Legalization Could Curb Mexican Drug Cartel Violence - Forbes (2011)

* Doctors advocate rescheduling Marijuana so more research can be done - LA Times (2009)

Dedicated to my mom and sister for your love and support and to my uncle Bobby, may this book answer your question.

Table of Contents

Forward

Dementia and My Aunt Elouise

"A good laugh is better than a dose of medicine" she would always say to me quoting from the Bible. Aunt Elouise was like my second mom. In fact, she was like another mother to more than a few in my family. Her love was unwavering. She worked all her life, even into her retirement. A breast cancer survivor, she passed away less than two years ago from complications of a stroke. Years prior to her death, she began losing mental capacity...misplacing her keys multiple times a day, staring at the TV screen, not able to drive anymore etc. It was devastating and heartbreaking to see her suffer. Seeing her frustration at the loss of her independence, considering she had always been the rock in our family. She was powerless over her medical condition. We don't know if it was dementia or Alzheimer's because the doctor wouldn't diagnose it, unwilling to prescribe another drug as she was already taking blood pressure medication and a couple of other prescriptions. Hearing something about marijuana helping with dementia, I often wondered if there had been a natural

cannabis medication, could it have improved the quality of her life in her last years. I also dedicate this book to my aunt Elouise and her loving memory.

Intro

ganja: noun, adj., smoking the leaves and plant tops of marijuana, smoked marijuana

Ganja Millionaire is about Cannabis. Specifically, ***Cannabis Sativa L*** plant species from which we get both industrial hemp (male plant) and marijuana (female plant). Marijuana, known by many names around the world, is arguably the most controversial plant on Earth. What is sure, marijuana is the most widely used illicit drug in the world and the number one cash crop in the U.S., over corn and wheat, estimated at over $36 billion annually.

The principal difference between hemp and marijuana is that hemp has virtually no THC and marijuana can have anywhere from 5 - 25% THC. We'll discuss THC later in the book. Another significant difference between hemp and marijuana is that hemp is used for food, health, and industrial purposes while marijuana is used for social, religious and medicinal purposes.

Coincidentally, you may have heard a lot about marijuana lately in the news and wonder what all the hoopla is about. You may ask yourself, like I did why this plant ignites such strong passions among both proponents and opponents of marijuana alike. Especially among what I call the *cannagencia,* consisting of patients, industry players, research scientists, doctors, lawyers and industry watchdogs (including enforcement) who know more about cannabis and the debate surrounding it than the average citizen.

> "I know nothing except the fact of my own ignorance" - Socrates

What I did not know about hemp and marijuana fills this book. It was very humbling to realize how little I knew about a plant I have *known* since my teens. **Ganja Millionaire** reflects what I learned. It is meant to be informative and beneficial in promoting a true historical perspective about this plant, uses and benefits and about the opportunities that exist today and potentially in the future concerning industrial hemp and medical marijuana. Hopefully the knowledge contained herein will increase awareness about cannabis that assists citizens, legislators, entrepreneurs and businesses of the United States and the world in making informed decisions about industrial hemp and/or medical marijuana should such legislation come before them in their respective states or countries.

In this book, best effort is made to just tell the story and refrain from unproductive finger-pointing, placing blame and alleging conspiracies as to why weed is illegal. My goal is to build bridges, not set them on fire.

For the record, I do not encourage nor promote marijuana use. In my opinion, the decision about cannabis use is a personal decision that should be made between adult patients and their physicians in states and countries where its use is not prohibited by law, international convention and/or treaty.

About the Author

Kenwa Jabuki grew up "*the skinny kid with glasses*" to a single mom, a long-time federal employee and his stepfather, a former police officer. Kenwa became a Series 3 licensed commodities trader at 20 years old, has jumped out of an airplane at 15,000ft and argued a case in a court of law as a layman at law!

In 2006, he started Houseof420.com, a marijuana themed t-shirt website with two UC Santa Cruz students assisting as models. In 2007, House of 420 became a social network and has since become the one of the fastest growing marijuana themed websites in the world.

Contact Kenwa

Do you have a personal story about hemp or marijuana, product, service, idea, feedback, cannabis history etc. you'd like to share? Kenwa would like to hear from you. For book signings and interview requests, also contact:

Email: kenwa@houseof420.com

Facebook: facebook.com/kjabuki

K. Jabuki c/o H420 Media 588 Sutter, #320 San Francisco, CA 94102

Can I Really Become a Ganja Millionaire?

My answer is unequivocally, absolutely, Yes, Yes, Yes!

Exciting opportunities exist, right now, in both the industrial hemp and medical marijuana industries in various parts of the world that can not only change your life financially, but also positively impact society. Whether its producing life-saving medicine, hemp farming, dispensing, providing an ancillary product or service that caters to the industry, generating tax revenue etc., the potential for individuals, corporations (including Big Pharma), cities, counties and governments to earn millions, if not billions, of dollars in these industries is truly staggering.

If you're like most people, before embarking on any career, business or investment opportunity, you want to know about the history of the industry, current industry climate and its growth and profit potential for the future. For those of you interested in careers and business opportunities in cannabis, this book should motivate, inspire and help prepare you for a path of success based on solid information about the industry upon which you seek to endeavor.

However I will not insult your sensibilities with reckless, pie in the sky claims. If success was easy, everyone would be successful. *Cannapreneurs* of the world will possess all the universal traits of hard work, sacrifice, ingenuity, perseverance etc. that embody professionals and innovators in other industries.

In the interest of full disclosure, the medical marijuana industry is experiencing some growing pains and the industrial hemp industry is non-existent in many countries even though hemp products are used worldwide. Personally, I foresee the medical marijuana industry overcoming these bumps in the road. Any new industry is going to have its share of compliance issues as industry players determine their roles and regulations are established. I view this as the natural evolution and selection of commerce that should eventually bring stability, credibility and longevity to this early stage industry. I also foresee the industrial hemp industry gathering steam in places where currently prohibited. Leaders of the free world have acknowledged, perhaps more vocally than ever, the need to reconsider existing drug policy, most recently at the 2012 Summit of the Americas in Cartagena, Columbia. Will you be ready? By reading this book, should you enter these gates, you can do so with your eyes wide open. Let's begin.

I. The Ancients & Cannabis

If you would understand anything, observe its beginning and
its development.
—Aristotle

The history of cannabis is truly fascinating and goes back to the first men and women of Earth, also known as *The Ancients*. It is important to note that cannabis was highly regarded by all ancient cultures and held to be one of the sacred herbs, "divine" or "magic plants." Through trial and error man discovered these divine plants, which led to worship, leading to the creation of deities, religion, and temples, and thus civilization.

In the ancient world, cannabis was used for medicine, food, drink, religious practices, and more. For thousands of years, hemp was the largest agricultural crop in the world. The fiber was used for clothing, rope and paper for both humans and domesticated animals. Sailcloth and rigging lines used for ships were all made from hemp as well.

The histories of man, civilization, and cannabis have something in common. They all can trace their beginnings back to the hub of civilization, the Four River Valley Civilizations, which includes:

- Ancient Africa (Nile River Valley)

- China (Yellow River Valley)

- India (Indus River Valley)

- Middle East Region (Tigris-Euphrates River Valley)

1

 ## Ancient Africa

The Origin of Cannabis

Cannabis originated in Africa and spread throughout the River Valley civilizations during the *migration out of Africa*. Some have contended that cannabis originated in China and made its way to Egypt via India. However cannabis was found in the royal tombs within the pyramids, which predate trade between Egypt and India by thousands of years. A more likely scenario is that the Ancient Chinese took cannabis with them when they left Africa. This assertion is based on an international, five-year study of the migration of modern man that found that Chinese people originated from early humans in East Africa. The research team, led by Jin Li of Fudan University in Shanghai, included researchers from Russia, India, Brazil, and other nations.

Ancient Ethiopia (Cush also Kush)

Ethiopia, known as *home of the gods* throughout the ancient world, is believed to home of the biblical Garden of Eden. Early evidence of cannabis smoking in Ethiopia dates back to the fourteenth century.

Ancient Egypt

The ancient Egyptians were a highly advanced civilization of over two million people spanning over six hundred miles. Egypt is most notable for the Nile River, the Great Sphinx, and the Great Pyramid, the last standing natural wonder of the world.

Ancient Egypt and Industrial Hemp

Hemp fiber was used to make rope that pulled the huge limestone blocks used to build the pyramids. Hemp was also used in the limestone quarries where dried hemp fiber was pounded into the cracks in the stone and wetted. The fiber would swell and help break the rock. The ancient Egyptian word for hemp was written in the Pyramid Texts.

Hemp material was found in the tomb of Pharaoh Akhenaten and traces of cannabis were found in the royal tombs of the pharaohs and nobility. Dr. Michele Lescott of the Museum of Natural History in Paris, France, and Dr. Svelta Balabanova, trained in forensic analysis, tested deep intestinal tissue from Pharaoh Ramses, the Great Godking, and found cannabis, coca, and tobacco.

"The ancient Egyptians certainly used drugs. As well as lotus, they had mandrake and cannabis," said Rosalie David, Curator of Egyptology at the Manchester Museum.

The ancient Egyptians including the Theraputea (origin of the word *therapeutic*) of Egypt used hemp, making it into clothing.

Ancient Egyptian Religious Rituals and Cannabis

Cannabis was sacred in the *Ntr Sentra* ritual practiced by the ancient Egyptians. Ntr Sentra, meaning "the breath of the divine," is thought to be among the world's oldest religious rituals. It is a ritual in which "divine smoke empowers and makes prayers more pleasing to the divine," according to Pr Ntr Kmt.

Ancient Egyptian Medicine and Marijuana

Ancient medicine evolved from magic and shamanism, back when illnesses were associated with demons and evil spirits in the body. Herbs were a large part of medicine in ancient Egypt. The excellence of Egyptian doctors was known all over the ancient world, and medical institutions called Houses of Life appeared in ancient Egypt as early as the First Dynasty.

"The practice of medicine is very specialized among them. Each physician treats just one disease. The country is full of physicians, some treat the eye, some the teeth, some of what belongs to the abdomen and others internal diseases" (Herodotus wrote of the Egyptians in *Histories* Book II, 84).

Imhotep

"The first figure of a physician to stand out clearly from the mists of antiquity" was Imhotep said Sir William Osler. I would be remiss to discuss ancient Egyptian medicine and not mention this legendary figure. The world's first multi-genius, Imhotep was a scribe, priest, philosopher, poet, astronomer and architect who built the first pyramid. Kings and queens even bowed before him. Imhotep, most notably was a healer and physician. Highly regarded as the universal father of medicine and ultimately deified as God of Medicine, the early Egyptians built the Temple of Imhotep, the world's first hospital, in his honor. The Greeks, well aware of his medical texts, praised him in inscriptions on Egyptian temples. He was worshipped in Greece and Rome for over 3000 years, his prestige increasing with the passage of time.

As a healer and doctor, Imhotep, knowing human anatomy and physiology, diagnosed and treated over 200 diseases, including arthritis, TB, gout, appendicitis and gallstones. Imhotep also performed surgery and practiced some dentistry.

Rosetta Stone

The Rosetta Stone, found in Egypt in 1799, was a decree issued by Pharaoh Ptolemy. It was written in hieroglyphics at the top, cursive hieroglyphics in the middle and had the Greek alphabet at the bottom. The decipherment of this stele in 1822, led the way for translation of other ancient Egyptians texts, steles etc.

Edwin Smith medical text is believed to have been written by Imhotep and is one of three ancient Egyptian medical texts, this one detailing cancer and surgical procedures including trauma surgery. Imhotep was adept at extracting medicine from plants.

Ebers Papyrus medical text, which recommends *"do thou nothing against",* is the first and oldest medical text prescribing cannabis for medical purposes, cannabis mentioned in the first line. Other plant medicines discussed include castor oil, aloe, frankincense, myrrh, opium and juniper. Many herbs, steeped in wine, were drunk as oral medicine. The most voluminous of the three texts, the Ebers papyrus is also a written code of ethics for the ancient Egyptian physicians describing accepted medical practices. The text also covers cancer treatment, mental disorders, depression, dementia, dentistry, digestive diseases, dermatology, traumatic diseases and more.

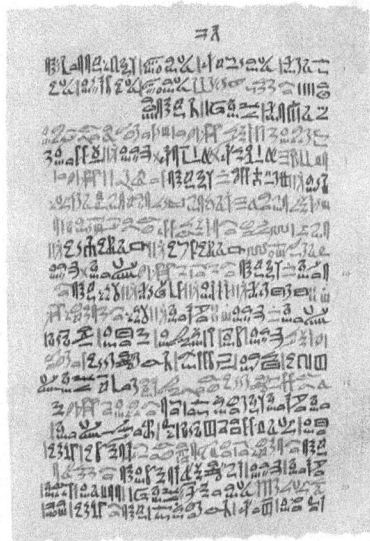

Kahun Medical Text is the oldest of the ancient Egyptian medical texts and discusses women's health in detail including pregnancy, fertility, contraception and gynecological diseases. The text also

5

outlines spiritual healings, massage and made extensive use of medicinal herbs, spices and foods.

Queen Seshat

"Seshat opens the door of heaven to you" - Coffin Texts, Spell 10

Goddess Seshat, the Enumerator, is a very interesting figure in ancient Egyptian history. She was either of nobility and/or a religious order in Egypt's Old Kingdom. Pharaoh Tuthmosis III nicknamed her *She of seven points*.

Her positions as *Overseer of Funerary Priestesses* and **Overseer of Female Physicians** were recorded on a stele. Her titles also included:

- Lady of Writings
- Head of the House of Divine Books
- Lady of Builders
- She Who Is Foremost in the Library

She acquired medical knowledge and climbed to the highest levels in medicine which like most scribal professions, was dominated by men.

Every cannabis grower knows the seven point symbol above Seshat's head bears a striking resemblance to a perfect marijuana leaf.

Modern Day Africa

Cannabis is known as bangue, dagga and riamba. Many tribes including Bergdama, Bashilange, Hottentotts, Kafirs, Senusis, Zulu's use marijuana medically for pain, tetanus, hay fever, convulsions, skin diseases, cholera and more.

Africa has a wide prevalence of cannabis use today. When the first white men went to Africa, they observed marijuana had been ingrained in native tradition and religious ceremonies in marijuana cultures throughout the continent for thousands of years. Visitors observed hemp cultivation and smoke from smoldering piles of hemp being inhaled by the African natives who were also known to use pipes. The African Dagga (marijuana) people believed cannabis was sent to earth by the gods.

The Bashilange tribe called themselves *Ben Riamba*, meaning *"the Sons of Hemp"*. Marijuana cultivation was a way of life for this religious group. They greeted one another with the word 'moio', meaning life and hemp. Devotion to the group by tribesmen was shown by smoking cannabis frequently and prior to battle or travel. The Bashilange believed marijuana has universal magic power to repel all evil. Peace treaties, trade agreements and holidays were not recognized without cannabis.

Cannabis is considered sacred and is connected with various religious and social customs in south central Africa. Some sects regard it as a magic plant symbolizing peace, friendship and offering protection against harm. Hemp use is a duty in some tribes.

Ancient China (Including Taiwan)

Cannabis, including both hemp and marijuana (also called *ma* or *dama*) has a rich history in China and has grown wild in nature there for thousands of years. The Ancients in China used cannabis as medicine, hemp seed for food and hemp fiber for clothing and cordage.

The ancient Chinese called their country "the land of mulberry and hemp" because of their high regard for hemp as a symbol of power over evil and to treat or cure the following ailments:

- prevent gray hair, hair loss and old age

- forgetfulness

- wound dressing

- menstrual disorders

- flesh firming

- post-partum

- poisoning

- vomiting

- ulcers

- constipation

- dry throat

- malaria

- Rheumatism and more...

Marijuana stalks with snake figures carved into them were used by ancient Chinese doctors. The doctor, standing over the sick patient, would raise the cannabis stalk and pound it on the bed commanding the demon to leave. The ancient Chinese marijuana stalk, some say, is the forerunner to modern medicine's sign of the staff with entwined serpents.

Fifth century Taoists also used cannabis with ginseng to gain advanced knowledge of future events and added it to incense burners believing its effects were a means of achieving immortality.

Around 100 A.D. the Chinese began using hemp to make paper. It is also around this time the early Chinese people began keeping written records detailing prescriptions for the medicinal use of cannabis, fully aware of its psychoactive properties. The oldest Chinese medical texts described the use, prescriptions and effects of marijuana:

* **Shénnóng Běn Cǎo Jīng** (ca. 100 CE) is the oldest Chinese pharmacopeia written by Emperor Shen Nong (shen meaning god; nong means agriculture), Father of Chinese Medicine. Emperor Nong who dedicated his life to agriculture, developed the science of curing with medicinal plants and taught hemp cultivation in 2800 B.C. He was ultimately deified. The *Shennong Bencaojing* specifically names cannabis (dama) as the "liberator of sin" and *mafen* "cannabis fruit-seeds".

Volume one of this medical text included 120 drugs harmless to humans

Volume two contains 120 therapeutic substances to treat the sick

Volume three, the last volume, discussed side effects and the toxicity of over 125 substances.

* ***Shiliao bencao*** *medical text* (ca. 730 CE) - prescribes daily cannabis use

* ***Zhenglei bencao*** *medical text* (ca. 1100 CE) - discusses effects of long-term cannabis use

Ancient Chinese shamans, known as *'wu'*, were magicians who used cannabis as a hallucinogenic drug. For most cultures, China included, medicine has its origins in magic.

Traditional Chinese Medicine has been in practice in China for thousands of years which includes the medicinal use of cannabis in addition to other herbs and lists cannabis as one of the 50 "fundamental" herbs. In fact, Traditional Chinese Medicine still represents forty percent of the health care provided in China today. The Chinese were very adept with this plant and used the entire plant medicinally:

- Cannabis flowers - recommended to treat wounds, menstrual disorders and over 120 diseases

- Achenia - prescribed to treat nervous disorders because of achenia's stimulative effect on the nervous system. Warned of possible hallucinations if used in excess.

- Cannabis seeds - eating these white kernels of the achenia regularly was believed by the ancient Chinese to firm the flesh and prevent old age. The seed are also consumed for tonic, diuretic and laxative issues. Used internally for vomiting, constipation, certain poisonings and post-partum issues among other uses. Externally prescribed for treating ulcers, hair loss and wounds.

- Cannabis oil was used for sulfur poisoning, dry throat and hair loss

- Cannabis leaves - the juice of the leaves was used for preventing grey hair, hair loss, scorpion stings and for its antiperiodic component.

- Cannabis stalk used as a diuretic

- Cannabis root and juice used as a diuretic and post-partum bleeding

Although marijuana was eventually outlawed in China thousands of years later, industrial hemp production has never been prohibited there as in Western countries. In fact, China is the world's largest producer of hemp, the land of mulberry and hemp.

Ancient India

In ancient India, cannabis was known as "sacred grass" "fountain of pleasures" "god's food" "hero leaved" "rejoicer" "joy" "Shiva's plant" and "desired in the three worlds"

Marijuana was associated with immortality according to Indian tradition. The churning of the Ocean of Milk, a creation myth relates cannabis to eternal life. In the leaves of the marijuana plant lived the angel of mankind says early Indian legends. Marijuana was so sacred, it was believed to repel evil and wash away the sins of its user.

Hemp is a holy plant in Hindu mythology as well, bestowed upon man for the "welfare of mankind" and is "considered to be one of the divine nectars able to give man anything from good health, to long life to visions of the gods." Nectar was defined as the fabled drink of the gods.

"Strive to move away from untruth towards truth"
-Atharva Veda

The **Atharva Veda** (*fearless knowledge*), a sacred text written between 2000 and 1400 BC, is the first Indian medical text. It lists cannabis as one of the "**Five Sacred Plants**" and as one of the five kingdoms of herbs. The **Atharva Veda** lists marijuana as a "sacred grass" "liberator" "source of happiness" and "joy-giver".

In ancient India, cannabis was used and classified three ways:

bhang - the leaves and tops of marijuana infused in beverage form and the preferred form of cannabis for use at religious festivals. Bhang was thought to be the favorite drink of Indra [King of Indian Gods] who in turn gave it to the people that they might achieve heightened states of consciousness, freedom of fear and joy.

ganja - smoking the leaves and plant tops of marijuana

hashish or *charas*- resin extract from marijuana leaves or the resinous buds from the plant

Siva, Supreme God of many Hindu sects, hemp plant was his favorite food earning him the title, Lord of Bhang.

In Northern India, cannabis is referred to as Sukha "peace-giver" by the Sikhs of Punjab and was used to aid in meditation and as a painkiller before battle.

The Buddha, "Siddhartha", ate and utilized only hemp and its seeds for six years before delivering his truths and becoming Buddha.

In the Tantric religion, based on a fear of demons, cannabis held an important place. Tantric believers sought protection in cannabis, and other plants, by setting them on fire to overcome evil, demonic forces. The Mahakala Tantra prescribes cannabis for medicinal use.

By the 10th century A.D., hemp was called indracanna meaning "the food of the gods". A later 15th century Indian writing described cannabis as "inspiration of mental powers", "speech-giving", "light-hearted', "joy-full" and "rejoices".

Modern India

Cannabis is still part of the meditative rituals performed in Tantric Buddhism in the Himalayas of Tibet and is taken at the Sikh and Hindu temples and Mohammedan shrines. Hindu ascetics, fakirs, view bhang as a method of communion with the divine and a way to prolong life.

India is one of the largest producers of hemp in the world. Cannabis has always grown naturally in India and industrial hemp production has never been prohibited in the country.

"...In the ecstasy of bhang, the spark of the Eternal in man turns into the light the murkiness of matter....Bhang is the Joy-giver, the Sky-filler, the Heavenly-Guide, the Poor Man's Heaven, the Soother of Grief...The supporting power of bhang has brought many a Hindu family safe through the miseries of famine. To forbid or even seriously restrict the use of so gracious an herb as the hemp would cause widespread suffering and annoyance and to large bands of worshipped ascetics, deep-seated anger. It would rob people of a solace on discomfort, of a cure in sickness, of a guardian whose gracious protection saves then from the attacks of evil influences..." - Indian Hemp Drugs Commission study on the use of hemp in India.

Ancient Europe

Cannabis in ancient Europe goes back as far as oral tradition during a time when the peasants used it for smoke or chew, medicine and rituals according to Nikolaas j. van der Merwe of the Dept. of Archaeology, University of Cape Town, South Africa.

Cannabis has been found in ancient Scythians tombs. Herodotus observed cannabis use among the Scythians in steam baths, noting, "the Scythians howl with joy for the vapour bath" (Herodotus IV:14). Scythians also used cannabis to cleanse themselves after funerals and as a way of honoring the memory of deceased leaders. They did this by placing hemp seeds on hot stones to produce thick smoke, then inhaling it and becoming intoxicated. Herodotus also noted the Thracians used it to make fine linens.

Ancient Greece

In ancient Greece, cannabis was used for nose bleeds, to expel tapeworms, inflammation and relief from pain. It was also used as veterinarian medicine to dress wounds and sores on horses.

Ancient Middle East

Mohammed (570-632 A.D.) did not specifically prohibit cannabis use though the use of alcohol was banned. Cannabis was considered a "Holy Plant" by the early Muslims and used as a sacred medicine by medieval Arab doctors which they called *kannab,* other names.

Arab doctors, in medieval times, prescribed cannabis for:

- Diuretic issues (help with urine flow)

- Nausea & vomiting

- Pain relief

- Seizures

- Anti-inflammatory

- Antipyretic (drug or herb to reduce fever)

The Sufis

A Muslim sect originating in 8th century Persia, the Sufis used hashish as a means to enhance esoteric consciousness and reverence of the nature of Allah. To the Sufis, eating hashish was an act of worship giving them deeper, otherwise unattainable, understanding and insight into themselves and wit. They also cited that hashish produced happiness, increased music appreciation and reduced both anxiety and worry. One Arab legend tells that Haydar, Persian founder of the Sufi religious order, encountered the cannabis plant in the Persian mountains one day while wandering, according to *Introduction to A Comprehensive Guide to Cannabis Literature* by Earnest Abel.

Ancient Iran

Back in ancient times, biblical time, Iran was known as Persia, located northeast to the ancient kingdoms of Babylonia, Assyria and Sumeria. Professor Mircea Eliade says, "Shamanistic ecstasy induced by hemp smoke was known in ancient Iran" suggesting that the Persian prophet Zoroaster, author of the Zend-Avesta, used hemp.

Zend-Avesta

In this ancient Iranian text, hemp is listed first among a list of 10,000 medicinal plants. In the Venidad "The Law Against

Demons", one of few surviving books of the Zend-Avesta, bhang (cannabis) is referred to a Zoroaster's' "good narcotic". The Venidad recounts a tale of two mortals whose souls were transported to the heavens where, after drinking a cup of bhang, the highest mysteries were made known to them. Professor Eliade postulates Zoroaster may have linked the metaphysical gap between heaven and earth with cannabis.

Ancient Japan

The ancient Japanese used hemp to cast out evil spirits and for purification ceremonies. The Shinto belief states purity and evil cannot coexist and thus Shinto priests by waving a gohei above someone's head would drive away evil spirits. A gohei was a short stick with un-dyed hemp fibers on one end. Hemp clothing was preferred at religious and formal ceremonies due to hemps ancient association with purity in Japan.

II. Marijuana and the Bible

"Behold, I have given you every herb bearing seed and to you it will be for meat" - Genesis 1:29

Cannabis was widely used during biblical times for incense, clothing, oil, rope, food, paper, sails and sealant and was used socially, in religion and as medicine.

The Wedding at Cana

The ancient Egyptians were early Christians. In Egypt, cannabis was made into a drink by steeping it in wine and then drinking it as an oral medicine for thousands of years before Christ. The word *'Cana'* appears in the Bible in the Book of John 2:1-11 as the first place Jesus performed a public miracle turning water into wine. *Cana* is derived from the same root word as cannabis. Coincidentally, in Sanskrit translations of the Old Testament Hebrew Bible, cannabis appears as *Cana.*

The Scythians, Zoroastrians and the Thracians, to name a few, were among groups that used cannabis during Jesus' time.

Cannabis and the Holy Anointing Oil: The Work of Dr. Benet

Dr. Sula Benet, a trained etymologist, has advanced some research concerning the biblical ties of cannabis that some consider quite controversial, even inflammatory in some religious circles. In the Book of Exodus, Moses receives the instructions, or recipe if you will, for making the *holy anointing oil*:

*Then the LORD said to Moses, 'Take the following fines spices,: 500 shekels of liquid myrrh, half as much of fragrant cinnamon, 250 shekels of **kaneh bosm**, 500 shekels of cassia - all according to the sanctuary shekel - and a hint of olive oil. Make these into a sacred anointing oil"* - Exodus 30: 22-33

Lost In Translation

Dr. Benet's ground-breaking research concentrated specifically on the interpretation of the herb **kaneh-bosim** appearing five times in the text of the Hebrew Bible and its relation to the religious use of cannabis. According to Dr. Benet, *kaneh-bosm*, mentioned twice concerning the holy anointing oil, has traditionally been called calamus, sweet cane or fragrant cane in English texts. Dr. Benet determined the word *kaneh-bosm* is a reference to cannabis and was used by ancient Jews medicinally, in religious rites, and as an offering or sacrament.

There is general consensus that *"kaneh"*, used in Talmudic texts, refers to hemp fibers not marijuana. Dr. Benet clarifies it is when the word *kaneh* appears with *bosm*, **kaneh bosm**, is it a reference to marijuana. Hebrew religious custom required the dead be buried in hemp shirts because of its association with purity.

If cannabis was part of the holy anointing oil, it was the third psychoactive ingredient. Frankincense and myrrh, ingredients in the holy oil as well, also possessed medicinal and psychoactive properties.

III. Cannabis in the United States

Marijuana is Americana

Make no mistake; cannabis has a deep rich history in the United States. Both hemp and marijuana are as American as baseball and apple pie. When the first European settlers arrived in the U.S. in the 1600's, they brought cannabis with them, began farming it and used it for almost everything.

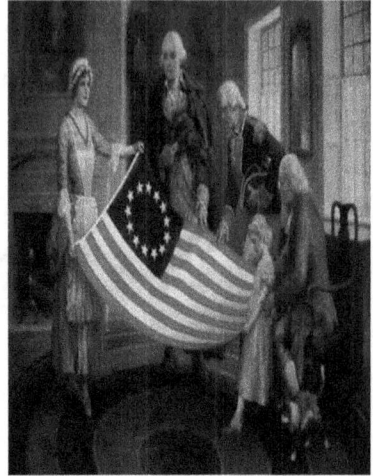

- For 200 years, hemp was legal tender in America and settlers could pay their taxes with it.

- America's first cannabis law was a mandate on farmers in Jamestown Colony, Virginia to grow hemp or risk fine or jail.

- Several states followed Virginia's lead and established similar laws requiring settlers to grow hemp.

- Drafts of the Declaration of Independence and the Constitution were written on hemp paper

- The U.S. flag, Stars & Stripes, was made with hemp fabric

- Ben Franklin started one of America's first hemp paper mills

- Bibles were printed on hemp paper

- Schoolbooks were printed on hemp paper

- Quality paints and varnishes were made with hemp oil

- Fine art was painted on hemp canvas

- By law, U.S. Government papers were written on "hempen rag paper" until 1920's

Weed and the War of 1812

Russia was the world's largest producer of the highest quality hemp, supplying 80% of Western hemp rope. The United States joined the war with Great Britain in 1812 over free-trade access to Russian hemp.

Marijuana and Modern Medicine

American doctors have long known of the medicinal value of marijuana. Prior to the advent of aspirin and pharmaceutical medicines, cannabis extracts and derivatives were the top prescribed medicines in the United States. From the 1800's until prohibition in 1937, doctors prescribed variations of *Cannabis Indica* and *Indian hemp* for:

- Infants

- Adults

- Veterinarian purposes including horses

The United States Pharmacopeia listed marijuana as a medicine from 1850 until 1942.

Weed Candy

The Ganjah Wallah Hasheesh Candy Company made a very popular candy in the U.S. containing cannabis derivatives and maple sugar. For over forty years, it was sold in in Sears & Roebuck catalogs and over-the-counter.

✿ IV. Growing & Blowing: Cannabis is Presidential!

"Early letters from our founding fathers refer to the pleasures of hemp smoking" - Dr. Burke of the American Historical Reference Society

What do the men on the one, two and hundred dollar bills have in common? They all grew hemp! Two of them were U.S. Presidents.

Puff, Puff, Pass...

George Washington, Thomas Jefferson, James Madison, James Monroe, Andrew Jackson, Zachary Taylor and Franklin Pierce were presidential cannabis smokers, says Dr. Burke, also a Smithsonian Institute consultant.

Jackson, Taylor and Pierce, being military men, also smoked it with their troops, Dr. Burke explains, improving morale no doubt. Pierce noting marijuana was "about the only good thing" about the War of 1848 in a letter to his family.

George Washington

During Washington's time, industrial hemp was still referred to as *hemp* but marijuana was now called *Indian hemp*. President Washington made the first and only admission at the presidential level that marijuana has value when he said, "...*Indian Hemp*...is *more valuable* than the common hemp". He also grew hemp as his primary crop at Mount Vernon, had a preference for a pipe full of "leaves of hemp" over alcohol and was fond of the fragrance of hemp flowers.

"Make the most of the Indian hemp seed and sow it everywhere" - The Writings of George Washington Volume 33, page 270

Abraham Lincoln

President Lincoln used hemp seed oil to fuel his household lamps including the lamp he used when signing the Emancipation Proclamation. Lincoln was openly against prohibition which he viewed as an infringement on American ideals.

"Two of my favorite things are sitting on my front porch smoking a pipe of sweet hemp, and playing my Hohner harmonica."

Thomas Jefferson

President Jefferson believed strongly in the value of hemp, grew hemp and kept meticulous notes of his hemp cultivation in the Jefferson Diaries. He is said to have exchanged smoking blends with George Washington as personal gifts.

"The greatest service that can be rendered to any country is to add a useful plant to its culture"

"Hemp is of first necessity to the wealth & protection of the country."

"An acre of the best ground for hemp is to be selected and sewn in hemp and be kept for a permanent hemp patch" T.J.'s Garden Book

James Madison

President Madison credited hemp with giving him the insight to create a new, free and democratic society.

James Monroe

Author of the Monroe Doctrine, James Monroe started smoking cannabis while Ambassador of France and continued till age 73. Burke, Pot & Presidents, June 1975

John Adams

"We shall, by and by, want a world of hemp more for our own consumption."

Jimmy Carter

President Carter suggested reducing the criminal penalty for simple marijuana possession.

"Penalties against possession of a drug should not be more damaging to an individual than the use of the drug itself; and where they are, they should be changed. Nowhere is this clearer than in the laws against possession of marihuana in private for personal use... Therefore, I support legislation amending Federal law to eliminate all Federal criminal penalties for the possession of up to one ounce of marihuana."

Barack Obama

President Obama made history in 2009 when he announced a shift in U.S. drug policy stating his Administration would not seek arrest to medical marijuana patients in compliance with state laws. Some have mistakenly construed this shift to mean that all enforcement would cease.

Note: The three most recent U.S. Presidents have all admitted youthful experimentation with marijuana.

🍁 Ganja Millionaire Spotlight 1: State of Kentucky (1800's)

Rationale: In 1850, there were over 8200 hemp farms of over 2000 acres each in the United States and many smaller ones, according to the U.S. Census. One state stood out for its hemp production which provided a high quality of life for farm owners and even liberty to some.

Kentucky: The Bluegrass State

Hemp grew so well in the state of Kentucky, that it rose to rule hemp production in the U.S. for decades, long after eastern states had abandoned it as a viable crop.

"Slavery was necessary for the production of hemp" - James F. Hopkins: *A History of the Hemp Industry in Kentucky*

Slaves Grew the Hemp in Kentucky

Free states did not raise hemp or tobacco because of the intensive labor needed, slave labor. Hemp was so intertwined with slave labor that it was unflatteringly referred to as the "[n-word] crop," on the belief that no one else understood it or handled it as expertly as slaves. New York Times March 14, 1926 & JFH book

Slaves and hired hands preferred working hemp fields because they had daily production goals and if they finished their work before quitting time, they could get off early. Plus they received incentives to boost their output. They earned a penny a pound of hemp they harvested and 75 pounds was an honest days' work. However, some of the sturdier, more ambitious slaves could harvest 100 and even 200 pounds of hemp per day. If fact, over the course of a few seasons some slaves could, and did, earn their freedom working the hemp field!

A Kentucky man stated in 1836 that it was almost impossible to hire workmen to break a crop of hemp because the work was "very dirty, and so laborious that scarcely any white man will work at it," and he continued by saying that the task was done entirely by the slave labor. Among the slave, the men held a monopoly on all the tasks connected with the production of the fiber because, in the words of this observer, "Negro women cannot labor at hemp at all..." (The Farmers' Register, III (1836), 612). Another commentator a few years later concluded that "none but our strong able Negro men can handle it to advantage."

Abolition of Slavery: Kentucky's fall from the Throne

U.S. hemp production began to decline long before prohibition actually banned it as a crop. In 1863 the Emancipation Proclamation, issued by President Abraham Lincoln, effectively ended slavery in the Southern states. The Proclamation infuriated both white and African-American slave owners who believed slavery was a state's rights issue and that the federal government, by abolishing slavery, was operating outside the scope of its' authority.

The Civil War and the Buffalo Soldiers

Another blow to the Kentucky hemp industry was the enlistment of African-Americans, both slave and free, into the United States Colored Troops (USCT), a U.S. Army regiment later known as the Buffalo Soldiers. As the Civil War progressed and white enlistment in the Union military slowed, thousands of African-Americans were recruited and served. Kentucky was second only to Louisiana in the number of Blacks that joined the USCT to serve their country. Kentucky Governor Thomas E. Bramlette and other Unionist Kentuckians were angered by the enlistments but unable to stop them.

Lack of Cheap Farm Labor Causes Economic Downturn

The end of slavery, some thought in Kentucky, would lead to financial ruin. Military enlistment of slaves and freemen and a 1865 federal policy making the wives and children of enlisted USCT free, caused the Kentucky slave numbers and thus the economy in Kentucky to collapse as many had feared. **Hemp production crashed eighty percent**, tobacco dropped fifty-seven percent and wheat production fell sixty-three percent. Finding replacement farm workers proved a daunting task and the machinery that would have aided in harvesting hemp was decades away.

Kentucky Can Be Great Again!

In January 2012, Industrial Hemp Legislation (House Bill 286) was introduced in the Kentucky State House of Representatives that could lay the foundation for industrial hemp to be grown once again in the Bluegrass State. Rep. Keith Hall, D-Phelps, a primary co-sponsor of the legislation is particularly interested in hemp diverse energy applications such as for automotive fuel etc.

Kenwa Jabuki

"Kentucky led the nation in its hemp production in the 1800's and there is every reason to believe we could do the same again if my bill becomes law," says Rep. Richard Henderson, D-Jeffersonville, a co-sponsor of the bill.

Kentucky Rep. Richard Henderson speaking, Agriculture Commissioner James Comer on left (AP Photo/ John Flavell)

"I am honored to join with Representative Henderson and so many of my former colleagues in support of legislation which could ultimately allow Kentucky farmers to produce industrial hemp," Kentucky Agriculture Commissioner James Comer.

Kentucky House of Representatives, Room 303, Sate Capitol Annex, Frankfort, KY 40601

Press release contact: Brian Wilkerson, email: <u>brian.wilkerson@lrc.ky.gov</u>

V. Pre-Prohibition: Understanding the Times

America: The Hot New Thing

Around the time slavery was ending, things really began to get going in the United States. Inventions and processes such as the cotton gin, mass production, airplane, radio, television etc. were revolutionizing the American way of life. America was growing and immigrants were flooding the States from all over the world. The US was emerging as a world power. The social dynamics as the country grew were equally fascinating.

Party in the USA (1850's - 1920's)

Even though the abolishment of slavery left some lingering resentment, Native Americans were being displaced and a clash with Mexican immigrants was going on out West, there was a rapid growth in American social culture. People were mingling across racial lines in many parts of the country. Jazz music and swing dancing were very popular at this time. The *'night life'* was in full swing. Folks were dressing up in fancy clothes and going to clubs to relax, socialize and listen to music. Marijuana at this time was also called gage, grifa, Mary Jane, Mary Warner, muggles, muta, rosa maria, reefer and tea.

Marijuana and Music

"It really puzzles me to see marijuana connected with narcotics . . . dope and all that crap. It's a thousand times better than whiskey - it's an assistant - a friend." - Louis Armstrong

Interestingly, some music legends sung about marijuana during the prohibition era. The songs below are relevant because they were written when state and federal laws were beginning to tighten on cannabis:

Willie the Weeper - Frankie 'Half Pint' Jaxon 1927 (the first reefer song)

Muggles (Instrumental) Louis Armstrong 1929

Reefer Man Cab Calloway & his Orchestra 1932

Reefer Man Baron Lee and the Blue Rhythm Band 1932

Gimme a Reefer Bessie Smith 1933

If You're a Viper Stuff Smith and his Onyx Club Boys 1936

When I Get Low, I Get High Ella Fitzgerald 1936

The Onyx Hop Frankie Newton and his Uptown Serenaders 1937

Reefer Hound Blues Curtis Jones 1938

Reefer Head Woman Jazz Gillum and his Jass Boys 1938

Smoking Reefers Larry Adler 1938

The times were pretty wild with gambling, prostitution and casinos. The prohibition on alcohol only fueled experimentation with other substances. Opium and heroin use was becoming a concern. Recreational use of cannabis, listed as a "fashionable narcotic" as early as 1853 (NY Times 1854), was enjoyed by mostly small niche groups all over the American landscape including east coast and southern blacks, bordellos in LA, among 'hip' whites, Mexican immigrants and soldiers fighting in the pacific expansion, WWI etc. Most Americans however had never heard of weed.

By the 1880's, almost 500 hashish parlors were open in NYC alone alongside the opium dens. These old school cannabis clubs were also frequented by a large number of men and women from "the better classes" according to Harper's Magazine (1883).

Hashish parlors also appeared in Boston, Chicago and Philadelphia.

Marijuana cigarettes, hand rolled cigarettes of tobacco and marijuana, were all the rage. The party atmosphere in the U.S. continued into what was known as the *Roaring Twenties*. However, during this time, government's views around the world, concertedly, were beginning to change about marijuana.

VI. Marijuana Prohibition (1850's - Present)

The Sphincter-Tightening on Weed...Putting the Stank On Dank

"A prohibition law strikes a blow at the very principles upon which our Government was founded." - Abraham Lincoln

Background

Attack Your Opponent's Strengths - Karl Rove Playbook: Tactic #2

After thousands of years of widespread, worldwide use for all manner of purposes, hemp and marijuana went from holy to hellish, divine to devil weed, medicine to poison, sacred to sinful and useful to useless, in short order. The long cherished cannabis plant which sustained the people of the Ancient world and modern times, morphed into an evil that had to be eradicated.

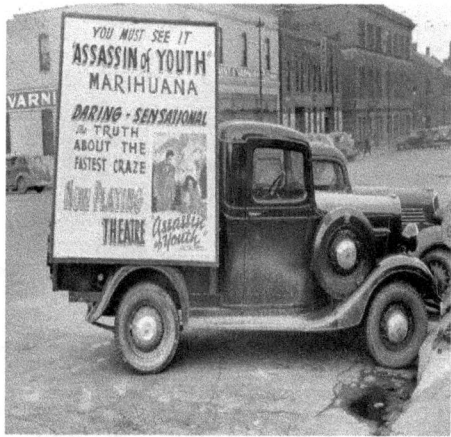

Laws in the U.S. and Britain began to place restrictions on marijuana around the time slavery ended, starting as regulations for doctors who prescribed it and as taxes on the user to generate revenue. Ironically, this in essence, is what is being proposed by marijuana advocates today.

The States Led the Way

By 1905, the USDA wrote that there were 29 states with laws that mentioned cannabis. These *poison laws* and *adulteration laws* as they were called, listed cannabis as a 'poison' and prohibited it from being mixed with other substances such as tobacco.

International Opium Convention (1925)

This was the first international drug control treaty to ban cannabis. The convention banned export of Indian hemp (marijuana) and its derivatives to countries that prohibited its use and required that any import be approved and "exclusively for medical and scientific purposes". The Convention was ultimately superseded by the Single Convention on Narcotic Drugs in 1961.

Giving Marijuana a Black Eye

Cannabis had become public enemy number one, "...more dangerous drug than heroin or cocaine." The legislation against marijuana was complemented by a media campaign consisting of print,

Beware! Young and Old — People in All Walks of Life!

This ▮ may be handed you by the friendly stranger. It contains the Killer Drug "Marihuana" — a powerful narcotic in which lurks *Murder! Insanity! Death!*

WARNING!

Dope peddlers are shrewd! They may put some of this drug in the ☕ or in the ⬚ or in the tobacco cigarette.

WRITE FOR DETAILED INFORMATION, ENCLOSING 12 CENTS IN POSTAGE — MAILING COST

Address: THE INTER-STATE NARCOTIC ASSOCIATION
(Incorporated not for profit.)
53 W. Jackson Blvd.   Chicago, Illinois, U. S. A.

film and highly inflammatory racial rhetoric that effectively turned people against marijuana and those who used it.

Yellow Journalism

"Marijuana, Assassin of Youth" - American Magazine 1937

As states imposed laws restricting cannabis, a flurry of newspaper and magazine articles began to associate every heinous crime and act of depravity with marijuana use. Sensational, attention grabbing headlines were used, often supported by little or no facts. A collection of like articles called the *Gore files* were later used at the congressional hearings to ban cannabis nationally.

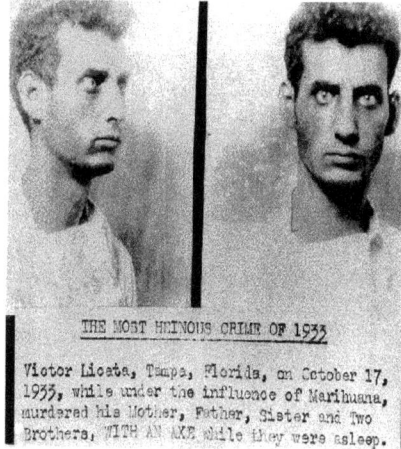

THE MOST HEINOUS CRIME OF 1933

Victor Licata, Tampa, Florida, on October 17, 1933, while under the influence of Marihuana, murdered his Mother, Father, Sister and Two Brothers, WITH AN AXE while they were asleep.

Panama Canal Zone Report

The Panama Canal Zone Report concluded there was no evidence that cannabis is habit forming and that it didn't have any "appreciably deleterious influence" on users. The report recommended no action be taken to prohibit its use by American soldiers in the Zone. (1925, reaffirmed 1933)

Reefer Madness

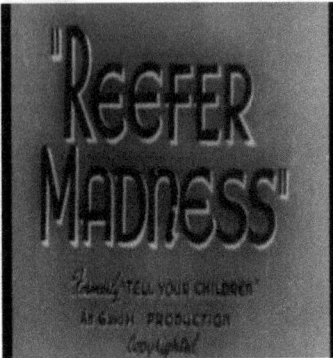

In 1936 a movie titled *Reefer Madness* was produced to warn parents of the dangers of marijuana. The movie called marijuana a "new and deadly menace" and the "burning weed with its roots in hell."

Dozens of different posters like the one on the right appeared on rail cars, buses, trains and street cars all over the U.S. promoting the Reefer Madness movie. Here's some more of what the public heard about weed in the movie:

"Marijuana is the most violence-causing drug in the history of mankind"

"Marijuana is an addictive drug which produces in its user's insanity, criminality and death"

Leads to "violence, murder suicide and hopeless insanity"

"You smoke a joint and you're likely to kill your brother"

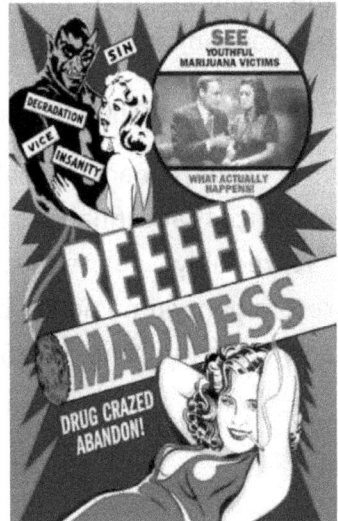

Marijuana Tax Act of 1937 - The War on Drugs

The Marijuana Tax Act was the first national cannabis legislation, consolidating the various state laws towards the ultimate federal prohibition of marijuana. Originally, the tax was conceived for the purpose of raising revenue, not officially make weed illegal. However the Act did for the first time in U.S. impose criminal penalties concerning cannabis for violations of the Act.

The Marijuana Tax Act implemented two fee structures:

$1,600 per ounce for personal use

* Under the Act, individual cannabis use for any 'undefined purpose' required registration with a doctor and a $100 per ounce tax. In 1937, $100.00 per ounce would be the same as paying $1,611.94 per ounce in 2012 (3.78%. annual inflation rate). Top quality medical marijuana retails for $350-$560 per ounce today so a $100 tax back in 1937 was far beyond the means of most marijuana users and thus prevented them from registering. Users began to seek cannabis from underground sources, which pursuant to the Act, was now a crime.

Doctors

* Individual cannabis use for specific, defined purpose required that a person register and pay a $1.00 per ounce tax. This tax was more than the actual price of the plant itself. As a result of the cost prohibitive tax, hassle of paperwork and controversy surrounding medical cannabis, doctors chose to prescribe other medicines.

The criminal penalty for unregistered, undefined use was:

1) Up to $2000 fine

2) Up to 5 years in prison

3) Possible tax evasion penalties

Because most quality paints and varnishes were made from hemp oil, Sherwin-Williams Paint Company opposed the Act and testified against it at the congressional hearing.

The American Medical Association, objecting to the taxes and fees it imposed on doctors and pharmacists, also opposed the Act and testified against it before Congress. Doctors were also threatened with imprisonment for pursuing cannabis research.

The Marijuana Tax Act passed in 1937, breaking ancient cultural ties to this plant.

Tougher Cannabis Laws

Over the next 30 years, subsequent laws stiffened the penalties including mandatory sentencing, increased punishment for cannabis possession and Three Strikes law.

Did You Know

In 1989, an ounce of weed cost more than an ounce of gold.

Marijuana and Prisons

Since prohibition began more than 10 million Americans have been arrested for marijuana with 87% for simple possession. Every 38 seconds someone is arrested for cannabis.

"The prestige of government has undoubtedly been lowered considerably by the prohibition law. For nothing is more destructive of respect for the government and the law of the land than passing laws which cannot be enforced. It is an open secret that the dangerous increase of crime in this country is closely connected with this." - Albert Einstein

Kenwa Jabuki

Ganja Millionaire Spotlight 2: Henry Ford

"Why use up the forests which were centuries in the making and the mines which required ages to lay down, if we can get the equivalent of forest and mineral products in the annual growth of the hemp fields?" - Henry Ford

Rationale: Today there are over 2 million cars on the road today with natural fibers including hemp in door panels, dashboards, seats, luggage racks etc. One innovator was deploying this technology over 80 years ago and had solutions for solving some of today's most pressing problems.

An idealist is a person who helps other people to be prosperous - Henry Ford

Henry Ford revolutionized industry when he pioneered mass production of automobiles in America. He grew hemp and manufactured plastics from renewable vegetable crops, including hemp. He, like the USDA, believed hemp production could help reduce the rate of deforestation of trees "centuries in the making". Mr. Ford was also working on a process to develop biofuels to reduce our carbon footprint and increase energy independence long before it was in the public discourse.

By 1929 Mr. Ford had begun extensive research into biomass derived fuels such as methanol. His process to make

these fuels would have reduced acid rain, greenhouse gases and dependence on fossil fuels.

The Original "Indestructible" Hemp Car

The Model T was made from hemp and built to run on hemp fuel. Henry Ford continued to improve on the use of hemp in his cars and in 1941, produced an automobile that was dubbed the "indestructible" car.

Popular Mechanics magazine ran a feature story on Henry Ford in December 1941. In the article was a picture of Mr. Ford with the car he "grew from the soil." The cars plastic panels had impact strength 10 times greater than steel and weighed a third less than its all steel competitors. The panels were made from natural fibers including flax, wheat, hemp, and spruce pulp. Because of prohibition and the Marijuana Tax Act, the hemp car never went into production.

Ford Motor Company, the company Mr. Ford founded, has the number one selling vehicle in the United States. Henry Ford, a true pioneer.

VII. USDA and Industrial Hemp

Monumental predictions were being made for industrial hemp at the same time laws were restricting cannabis. Leading magazines praised hemp's potential as a crop:

"The Most Profitable and Desirable Crop That Can Be Grown" - Mechanical Engineering Feb. 1937

"New Billion Dollar Crop...can produce more than 25,000 products, ranging from dynamite to Cellophane" - Popular Mechanics Feb. 1938

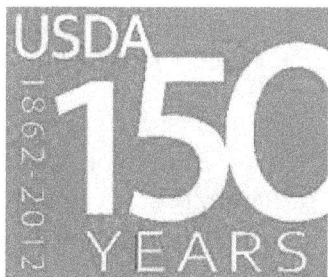

USDA and Mr. Lyster Dewey

The U.S. Dept. of Agriculture has conducted perhaps the most exhaustive, comprehensive research on industrial hemp than any other organization on the planet. For over 40 years, Lyster Dewey, a chief scientist and botanist at USDA, dedicated much of his professional life to the study of this plant. Mr. Dewey grew hemp for USDA study on government land called *Arlington Farms*. During WWII, a large portion of this land was annexed by the War Dept. to build the something called the **Pentagon.**

Mr. Dewey's meticulous hemp diaries containing extensive notes on hemp were recently discovered and bought by the trade group, Hemp Industries Association.

USDA Predicts Hemp Would Rule Again

From 1901 until the 1930's, USDA predicted machinery would be developed capable of harvesting hemp making it

America's number one crop again. Unfortunately, cannabis was banned before the machinery arrived on the scene.

Hemp and USDA Yearbook of Agriculture

In 1913, the entire *USDA Yearbook of Agriculture* was dedicated to the discussion of industrial hemp which spoke to USDA's serious and diligent study of this plant. The following year, hemp appeared on U.S. currency.

1914 $10 "Hemp Bill"

U.S. Federal Reserve note

USDA Predicts Hemp Paper to Reduce Deforestation

In 1916 USDA Bulletin #404 called for an expansion of hemp, predicting that all paper would be made from hemp by the 1940's eliminating the need to cut down trees. USDA studies showed one acre of hemp produced 4 times as much pulp as four acres of trees. USDA study also showed hemp produces a superior quality of paper that does not yellow nor deteriorate over time. Hemp paper can be recycled more than wood based paper.

USDA and Hemp Help Win the War!

When Japan cut off hemp from the Philippines during WWII, the U.S. temporarily lifted the ban on hemp production and USDA recruited American farmers to grow hemp. The recruitment

campaign was called *Hemp for Victory* and USDA produced a video to show farmers how to grow, harvest hemp and process. It was mandatory for farmers to attend a showing of the film. Special licenses were issued to farmers like the one below.

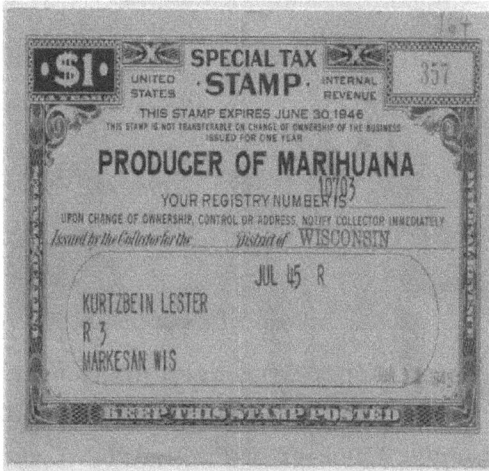

USDA provided hemp harvesting equipment at little or no cost and farmers and their sons were waived from military service if they grew hemp. When the war ended in 1945, the Hemp for Victory campaign was terminated. USDA has continued industrial hemp research well in the 1950's and perhaps the 1970's.

Happy 150th Birthday USDA!

VIII. Worldwide Renaissance: Hemp Making a Comeback

Free Enterprise: The Rise of Industrial Hemp Production

Industrial hemp is the male version of the cannabis plant. It has virtually no THC meaning you cannot get "high" on hemp. Most products which are made from cotton, wood or oil (including plastics) can be made from hemp. Apparel has been made from hemp since antiquity. Levi Strauss, Calvin Klein, Patagonia and Armani, to name a few, have made hemp blended apparel.

People are hurting all over the world by unemployment and the housing crisis. American cities are filing for bankruptcy; states are running huge deficits, countries in need of a bailout. Yet we have forbidden a plant with thousands of uses, industrial hemp. It is said the potential of the industrial hemp industry once the ban on production is lifted is over $500 billion dollars. People all over the world have their sleeves rolled up ready to unleash their ingenuity on this amazing plant. Some are doing so currently. And while allowing for hemp production will not solve the serious employment and financial problems we face, it could certainly help.

Benefits of Growing Industrial Hemp:

Creates Jobs & Opportunities

Industrial hemp creates jobs and business opportunities wherever it is grown.

Kenwa Jabuki

Cleaner Air with Hemp

Animal life could not exist without plants removing harmful CO_2 from the air. Hemp through a process called carbon dioxide sequestration, cleans the air of CO_2 [carbon dioxide] three times as more than trees. Carbon dioxide is a greenhouse gas that is known to contribute to global warming.

Environmentally Friendly

Hemp grows fast, organically without fungicides, pesticides or herbicides, keeps other weeds from growing, does not deplete the soil and does not harm the environment.

Sustainable Energy Independence

Dept. of Energy says hemp as a biomass fuel such as cellulosed ethanol requires the least specialized growing and processing procedures of all hemp products. The possibility of adding hemp oil to crude oil and other oil based products, reducing the rate of depletion of crude oil reserves is promising.

Superfood: Hemp Seed and Hemp Oil is Healthy

Hemp is a versatile, protein packed, super food which contains all 10 essential fatty amino acids for a healthy metabolism. Hemp is also rich in Omega-3 and Omega-6, including Gamma Linolenic Acid (GLA) to help maintain healthy cholesterol and blood pressure levels. Hemp has anti-inflammatory properties, lubricates the arteries, may lower heart attack risk and help the immune system. Hemp seed is lowest in saturated fats than other vegetable oils such as canola and soybean. Hemp foods are vegan friendly, kosher, easy to digest and are not genetically modified.

The World Health Organization states the ideal ratio of Omega-6 to Omega-3 is 4:1, the hemp ratio is 3.75:1.

- Can be made into delicious, flavored milk shakes
- Can be spiced to taste like meat such as chicken, steak or pork;
- Can be sprouted for salads, ground into meal, and also made into margarine.
- Hemp oil is good for the skin and beauty products
- Lowers cholesterol
- Washed hemp seed has no THC
- Can produce a tofu-like curd
- Hemp seed is a nutritionally balanced food for domestic pets and farm animals.

Hemp Exchange Traded Futures Contracts & Options

If the international treaties and conventions were amended to allow for hemp production, listing hemp as a contract on one of the exchanges in Chicago, Kansas or New York would allow producers to sell and hedge prices on the world market. Trading would be open to speculators as well.

Domestic (U.S.) Hemp contract (15,000 ton contracts)

World Hemp contracts (40,000 ton contracts)

Ganja Millionaire Spotlight 3: Hemcrete

Rationale: What do the pyramids in Egypt and the Great Wall of China have in common? They were all built using hemp & limestone and are still standing! These materials are experiencing a rebirth as viable construction and building products.

hemcrete

Tradical® Better-than-zero carbon

Tradical® Hemcrete®is a bio-composite building material made from hemp shiv (the woody core of Industrial Hemp) and a lime based binder called Tradical® HB. Tradical® Hemcrete®is made and sold in the UK by Lime Technology under license from Lhoist.

Tradical Hemcrete possesses the following properties:

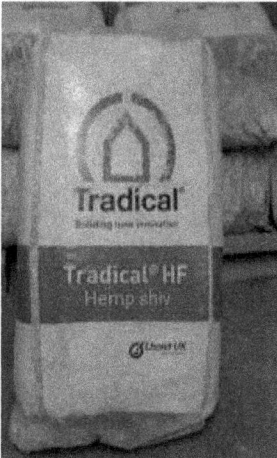

- Good thermal insulation
- Excellent thermal inertia
- Negative embodied carbon
- Easy to use
- Made from renewable/abundant UK materials

Tradical® Hemcrete® is normally used to create the walls of new buildings and can used in the refurbishment of existing buildings. The average life span for Hemcrete buildings is 700 year.

In the U.S., American Lime Technology (Chicago, IL)

Ganja Millionaire Spotlight 4: Kevin McCloud & the United Kingdom

Rationale: The U.K. and one man in particular are at the forefront of developing sustainable living.

"HAB Oakus is a joint venture between Kevin McCloud's HAB development company and housing group GreenSquare. They design places and homes that "respect local context and biodiversity, where residents feel a strong sense of belonging". Haboakus mission is sustainable living and homes that are "environmentally efficient to build and run."

Kevin McCloud's revolutionary sustainable housing scheme completed

The Triangle in Swindon is a sustainable 42-home rural housing development developed by HAB Oakus featuring Tradical® Hemcrete®. The scheme was completed as part of the UK's Homes and Communities Agency's Renewable House Programme and the site was visited by Housing Minister Grant Shapps.

Prime Minster David Cameron officially opened Blackditch, Stanton Harcourt which is another development by HAB Oakus featuring Tradical® Hemcrete®. The two visits have reinforced the UK Government's commitment to supporting the use of renewable materials.

The Low Carbon Agenda

The Government's UK Low Carbon Transition Plan was announced in 2009 which initially aimed to build 60 or more low-carbon, affordable homes using innovative, highly insulating, renewable materials. The new scheme aims to demonstrate the viability of these materials and act as a spur for the renewable construction materials industry. It is also helping to engage the affordable housing sector in the low-carbon agenda. - Homes and Communities Agency's website

Ganja Millionaire Spotlight 5: Push Designs

Anthony Brenner, Founder & Lead Designer

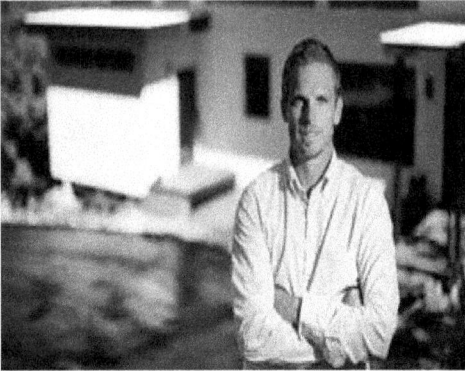

America's First House Made of Hemp!

America's first house made primarily of hemp has been built in 2010 using Tradical® Hemcrete®. Push Design and a team of 40 volunteers, sub-contractors and designers completed construction of the hemp house located in Ashville, North Carolina. Push Design, an eco-friendly design and construction company has gained the support of community members and local officials alike and now plans to build more.

"We are a progressive values-based company — family, health, social equity and environ-mental responsibility are at the core of every project we engage and every decision we make... We are always seeking new like-minded clients, part-ners and investors to join us in our efforts to revolutionize the building and development industries and make the world a better place for our children" said Mr. Brenner

"The fact that the lime content is constantly calcifying, turning to stone essentially, over the wall's life span, means the wall is actually getting harder and stronger as time goes on," David Mosrie of Push Design said. "The durability is unlike anything we have seen, with the exception of stone, as perhaps even beyond that as there is no mortar joint failure possible. Studies in Europe have estimated about a 600-800 year life span for the wall system."

Mr. Mosrie adds "The main negative effect of the legal situation [in the U.S] is the cost to import it...Local production would not only lower the environmental impact exponentially versus bringing it from Europe, but would bolster a struggling economic group and prop up local farming, a long regional tradition." Everyone should live in a home built of health, beauty and integrity.

Ganja Millionaire Spotlight 6: Lotus Elise 2013

Rationale: One respected car maker is using hemp to help reduce the global carbon footprint and increase vehicle safety. All this is accomplished without compromising style, or performance.

Famed car manufacturer, Lotus Engineering, is well known for its' exotic high performance automobiles. Company founder Colin Chapman's philosophy of building cars is performance through light weight.

In 2008 Lotus pushed the engineering envelope again with the introduction of the stylish, head-turning **Eco Elise** featuring hemp composite parts and other natural fibers.

Built in the countryside, the Eco Elise is a hemp based, "green", high performance sports car. Specifically, Lotus chose hemp for the body panels, rear spoiler and hemp is utilized in the manufacture of the seats. These body parts, made from local materials, absorb CO_2 in addition to providing an attractive and durable finished product.

Lotus, by incorporating hemp instead of fiberglass, is able to reduce the Eco Elise's carbon footprint while actually strengthening the integrity of the hemp infused parts.

The 2013 Lotus Elise is powered by a 134bhp Toyota engine, reaches 0-60 mph in 6 seconds, gets 46 mpg and produces very little emissions. The hemp composite parts in the award winning Lotus Elise are grown locally, provide a strong material for the car and is a "beautiful material to look at" said Lee Preston of Lotus Engineering.

Hemp isn't the only natural fiber in this "green" car. The seats, steering wheel boss and door cards in the Eco Elise are covered in dye-free fabric made from locally reared Norfolk sheep. The paint on the Elise is an oil-free water-based lacquer.

Lotus has also attached a pair of solar panels to the roof made from fully biodegradable hemp which runs the stereo and air conditioning systems, meaning less work for the alternator and thus using less fuel.

Honorable Mention: Kesler

IX. Marijuana - The Great Revelation

When I obtained my cannabis card for the first time and began going to dispensaries, marijuana was being referred to as "medicine" and consumption was called "medicating". How clever I thought to myself, smiling every time I heard it. "I'm going to get my medicine" I would say grinning from ear to ear. Little did I know at the time, the connection between cannabis and medicine is true and pure. Sure I had heard tidbits here and there about marijuana being good for some things. However I had no idea of its historical significance worldwide, the encouraging and growing volume of modern medical and scientific cannabis research and the depth of its known and potential benefits.

It has been reported marijuana contains over 300 compounds. I always thought the implication was that all of these compounds were harmful and dangerous. However it turns out, at least 85 of these compounds, and counting, called *cannabinoids,* form the basis for medical and scientific study of cannabis.

Cannabinoids

Marijuana is the only plant genus on the planet that contains these medicinal *cannabinoids* which work as antiemetic's for vomiting & nausea, appetite stimulants, antispasmodics (for muscle spasms) and pain relievers (analgesics) for migraines and more.

The Big 3

Three of these cannabinoids are generating most of the interest because of their enormous potential and known medical applications in the treatment of a wide range of ailments:

THC ($C_{21}H_{30}O_2$) aka Delta9-Tetrahydrocannabinol, the **primary compound** in marijuana, has medicinal and psychoactive effects. The compound, a mild analgesic, has also demonstrated antioxidant properties. A synthetic, pharmaceutical grade of THC called Dronabinol (Marinol) became available in the U.S. in 1985.

Cannabidiol aka [CBD], CBD is a major, non-psychoactive compound in marijuana representing up to 40% of extracts from the plant. Relieves nausea, cough and congestion, anxiety, inflammation, convulsion and may inhibit cancer cell growth. Marijuana with high CBD content may be particularly helpful to people who suffer from multiple sclerosis, Tourette syndrome, and frequent panic attacks. CBD works against THC's psychoactive effect.

Cannabinol aka [CBN] - this therapeutic cannabinoid found in marijuana is a metabolite, or by product, of THC.

Ganja Millionaire Spotlight 7: U.S. Government

Dept. of Health & Human Services

Rationale: The U.S. government knows more about marijuana than most of us. The U.S. Army used it as a truth serum in the 1940's and Uncle Sam currently provides weed to a handful of patients. The U.S. government also grows weed, is the largest funding source for marijuana research in the world, has commissioned many studies of the plant and appears to have found it to possess significant medicinal properties.

FREE WEED! U.S. Govt. v. Robert Randall

In 1976, Robert Randall, a glaucoma patient, sued the U.S. govt. after he was charged with marijuana cultivation (*Randall v. U.S.*). Mr. Randall won. The judge ruled, in part..."*no adverse effects from the smoking of marijuana have been demonstrated. Medical evidence suggests that the medical prohibition is not well-founded.*"

Randall filed a petition in May 1976 and began receiving FDA-approved medical marijuana. As a result of Randall's case, the *Compassionate Investigational New Drug* program was created by the FDA and at its peak, allowed thirty people to receive medical marijuana. The program was closed by the Bush Administration in 1992 and the participating patients were grandfathered in.

In 2006, there were seven remaining patients who get eight or nine ounces of marijuana per month. The medicine is provided in tin cans consisting of 300 pre-rolled cigarettes per can which is sent pharmacists for pick up by the patients.

U.S. Govt. Grows Marijuana!

The medical marijuana provided for the *Compassionate Investigational New Drug* program is grown by the Univ. of Mississippi (Oxford) under federal contract administered by *National Institute on Drug Abuse (NIDA)*. Ole Miss has grown the weed for Uncle Sam since 1968 and provides it to licensed researchers and universities in the U.S. studying marijuana under contract from NIDA.

U.S. Govt. Patents Medical Marijuana!

Here's where the grits get a lil thick. The U.S. government patents things all the time. There is nothing unusual about that. However, it is Uncle Sam's medical patent on weed, while still listing it as *having no medical value* in the Controlled Substances Act, that has the whole world abuzz and medical marijuana advocates dumbfounded. U.S. patent law requires a patent to show "specific, substantial and credible value".

Govt. Patent Claims Marijuana Has Medicinal Value

The U.S. Dept. of Health and Humans Services (DHHS), on October 7, 2003, was awarded U.S. patent 6630507 entitled, "Cannabinoids as Antioxidants and Neuroprotectants". The patent is based on research conducted by National Institute of Mental Health (NIMH) and National Institute of Neurological Disorders and Stroke (NINDS).

The U.S. government patent asserts cannabinoids are:

"useful in the treatment and prophylaxis of wide variety of oxidation associated diseases, such as ischemic, age-related, inflammatory and autoimmune diseases. The cannabinoids are found to have particular application as neuroprotectants, for example in limiting neurological damage following ischemic insults, such as stroke or trauma or in the treatment of neurodegenerative diseases such as Alzheimer's disease, Parkinson's disease and HIV dementia"

Govt. Marijuana Patent Awarded to Private Firm

On November 17, 2011, DHHS and National Institutes of Health announced plans to grant exclusive patent license for U.S. patent 6630507 entitled, "Cannabinoids as Antioxidants and Neuroprotectants to *KannaLife Sciences.*

KannaLife website describes the company as a late stage, socially responsible, phyto-medical company specializing in the research & development of pharmacological products derived from plants including synthetic and patented cannabinoids.

X. Marijuana is a Medicinal Plant

This section is an accumulation of research by doctors, scientists, health professionals and government agencies, not my opinion or hope for what cannabis may do medically for patients. I do not embellish nor exaggerate the findings of their research. Marijuana has well-documented medically beneficial effects and is currently used in the treatment of the following:

Cancer

The world's leading cause of death. A total of 1,596,670 new cancer cases and 571,950 deaths from cancer were projected in the U.S. for 2011 says the American Cancer Society. Worldwide, 10 million new cases of cancer are diagnosed and 8 million deaths each year.

Cancer Drug Shortage

Fox News reported in early 2012 that cancer patients are dying due to a lack of cancer drugs. Dr. Sanjay Gupta reported on CNN in July 2012 that a half million Americans die each year due to the cancer drug shortage.

There is wide acceptance that marijuana helps with nausea and vomiting associated with chemotherapy. However, it is the contention that marijuana may have anti-cancer effects that sends folks into a tizzy. However this book would lack credibility if I didn't mention this information.

"Medical marijuana is becoming more and more associated with anti-carcinogenic effects which are responsible in preventing or delaying the development of cancer. This means that cannabinoids offer cancer patients a therapeutic option in the treatment of highly invasive cancers". - National Health Federation (NHF)

Reported Benefits:

Brain Cancer (Tumors) - Cannabinoids in marijuana such as THC help kill brain cancer cells through a process called autophagy, which helps the cells feed on themselves. A Spanish medical team in February 2000 found that THC shrinks tumors in lab rats. The study was led by Dr. Manuel Guzman of Complutence University of Madrid.

Breast Cancer - Cannabidoil may keep breast cancer from spreading through the body by blocking the Id-1 gene believed to cause metastasis which is the aggressive spread of cancer cells away from the original tumor site. The researchers, California Pacific Medical Center Research Institute, are hopeful their discovery may provide a non-toxic alternative to chemotherapy.

Leukemia, Breast & Lung Cancer - In 1974, a study by Medical College of Virginia found that THC in marijuana curbs the growth of three kinds of cancer in mice both benign and cancerous ..."THC slowed the growth of lung cancers, breast cancers and a virus-induced leukemia in lab mice and prolonged their lives..." according to an article that appeared in Washington Post August 18, 1974 headlined *"Cancer Curb Is Studied".*

The International Medical Verities Association is putting hemp oil on its cancer protocol, a prioritized protocol list of anti-cancer medicines, the top five including magnesium chloride, iodine, selenium, Alpha Lipoic Acid and sodium bicarbonate, all available without prescription. - NHF

Kenwa Jabuki

"The medical science is strongly in favor of THC laden hemp oil as a primary cancer therapy, not just in a supportive role to control the side effects of chemotherapy" - National Health Federation

Alzheimer's and Dementia

The Alzheimer's Association states 5.4 million Americans are living with Alzheimer's disease. One in eight older Americans has the disease which is the sixth-leading cause of death in the U.S. costing $200 billion for 2012.

Reported Benefits: "Cannabinoids are found to have particular application as neuroprotectants, for example in limiting neurological damage following ischemic insults, such as stroke or trauma or in the treatment of neurodegenerative diseases such as Alzheimer's disease, Parkinson's disease and HIV dementia" - U.S. Govt. patent

Also, Scripps Research Center in California conducted research showing THC, the primary active ingredient in marijuana, prevents an enzyme called acetyl cholinesterase from accelerating the formation of deposits called "Alzheimer plaques" in the brain more effectively than commercially available drugs.

Arthritis

Arthritis affects approximately 49 million people in the U.S. costing an estimated $80 billion in medical costs and $40 billion in lost wages. Arthritis is an Immune System Disorder in which the immune system overacts to perceived bacterial threats creating uncontrolled inflammation, fever and infections.

Reported Benefits: THC in marijuana reduces nausea and pain associated with inflammation. THC also provides immune system suppressant factor when used in conjunction with medications such as Enbrel [TM] or as an alternative adjunctive therapy.

Glaucoma

Glaucoma is a complicated disease in which damage to the optic nerve leads to progressive, irreversible vision loss and is the second leading cause of blindness according to the Glaucoma Research Foundation. It is estimated that over 2.2 million Americans have glaucoma but only half of those know they have it.

Reported Benefits: The THC & cannabigerol found in marijuana reduces the pressure within the eye also called intra-ocular pressure (IOP). A review of studies by the Institute of Medicine of glaucoma patients and healthy adults showed a reduction of IOP by 25% on average after smoking a marijuana cigarette with 2% THC content.

Multiple Sclerosis (MS)

Muscle spasms in MS patients "are the hallmark of the debilitating autoimmune disease" according to US News. There are about 250,000 - 350,000 people with MS in the U.S. with 200 new cases each week.

Reported Benefits: CBD and THC extracts reduce spasticity in treating multiple sclerosis (MS) related muscle spasticity. This is according to six controlled, randomized trials of treated patients. "Spasticity, an involuntary increase in muscle tone or rapid muscle contractions, is one of the more common and distressing symptoms of MS," the researchers noted in their review," said lead researcher Dr. Shaheen Lakhan, executive director of the Global Neuroscience Initiative Foundation.

"The therapeutic potential of cannabinoids in MS appears to be comprehensive, and should be given considerable attention," Dr. Lakhan added also noting "cannabinoids may provide neuroprotective and anti-inflammatory benefits in MS."

Research into marijuana's potential to slow MS progression & control tremors of MS patients as well is ongoing.

Parkinson's disease

A degenerative neurological disorder that affects approx. 500,000 people in the U.S. suffer from the disease with around 50,000 new cases reported annually.

Reported Benefits: "Cannabinoids are found to have particular application as neuroprotectants, for example in limiting neurological damage following ischemic insults, such as stroke or trauma or in the treatment of neurodegenerative diseases such as Alzheimer's disease, Parkinson's disease and HIV dementia" - U.S. Govt.

Nearly half of Parkinson's disease patients report that cannabis helps relieve their symptoms according to a study of patients.

Medical Cannabis, according to studies, may also be useful in treating: asthma, depression, digestive diseases, leukemia, epilepsy, PTSD, Tourette syndrome, psoriasis, sleep apnea, Hepatitis C, Bi-polar Disorder, Anorexia Nervosa and more.

Neurogenesis: This Is Your Brain on Marijuana

"Only marijuana promotes neurogenesis" - Dr. Xia Zhang, Univ. of Saskatchewan

Neurogenesis is the birth of neurons (brain cells) in the brain, a process most active in pre-natal development but that continues throughout adulthood. Many of these neurons die at birth but a number of them survive and become functional and integrated into the brain tissue. A global research team from US, Canada and China led by Dr. Xia Zhang, Univ. of Saskatchewan, found that cannabinoids found in marijuana promote neurogenesis and produce anti-depressant effects. Most drugs of abuse such as opiates, nicotine, alcohol, cocaine etc. suppress neurogenesis.

Can I Overdose on Marijuana?

"Nearly all medicines have toxic, potentially lethal effects. But marijuana is not such a substance. There is no record in the extensive medical literature describing a proven, documented cannabis-induced fatality. In practical terms, marijuana cannot in duce a lethal response" - U.S. Dept. of Justice approved statement 1998

"In strict medical terms, marijuana is far safer than many foods we commonly consume. It is physically impossible to eat enough marijuana to induce death. Marijuana, in its natural form is one of the safest therapeutically active substances known to man" - Francis L. Young, Administrative Law Judge, DEA

"The evidence is overwhelming that marijuana can relieve certain types of pain, nausea, vomiting and other symptoms caused by such illnesses as multiple sclerosis, cancer and AIDS or by the harsh drugs sometimes used to treat them. And it can do so remarkably safely. Indeed, marijuana is less toxic than many of the drugs that physicians prescribe every day" – Former U.S. Surgeon General in an Editorial in Providence Journal March 26, 2004

XI. Smoked Marijuana: The Poor Man's Health Care

The Skinny on Smoking a Fatty

It is interesting to note that most people I know who smoke marijuana do not have health care. However, there is conflicting information concerning 'smoked' marijuana:

"Marijuana smoke is a crude THC delivery system that also sends harmful substances into the body' - ONDCP

"Estimates suggest that from 20 to 50 million Americans routinely, albeit illegally, smoke marijuana without the benefit of direct medical supervision. Yet despite this long history of use and the extraordinarily high number of social smokers, there are simply no credible reports to suggest that consuming marijuana has caused a single death. By contrast, aspirin, a commonly used, over-the-counter medicine causes hundreds of deaths each year." - DEA Administrative Law Judge Francis L. Young

"Consumer Reports believes that for patients with advanced AIDS and terminal cancer, the apparent benefits some derive from smoking marijuana outweigh any substantial or even suspected risks - Consumer Reports editorial 1997

"There is very little evidence that smoking marijuana as a means of taking it represents a significant health risk. Although cannabis has been smoked widely in the Western countries for more than four decades, there have been no reported cases of lung cancer or emphysema attributed to marijuana. I suspect a day's breathing in any city with poor air quality poses more of a threat than inhaling a day's dose which for many ailments is just a portion of a joint. - Emeritus Professor of Psychiatry Harvard Medical School *"Puffing Is the Best Medicine"* LA Times May 5, 2006

UCLA Study on Smoking Marijuana

Smoked marijuana is the fastest way to receive the plant's medical benefits which, curiously, are up to three times more powerful when smoked versus other methods of dosing. The David Geffen School of Medicine at UCLA, led by Dr. Donald Tashkin conducted the largest study on this and unexpectedly found no connection between smoking marijuana and cancer.

Dr. Tashkin, a pulmonologist, who has studied marijuana for 30 years, hypothesized there would be a positive link between marijuana use and lung cancer. "What we found instead was no association at all, and even a suggestion of some protective effect" he says. His study was funded by National Institute of Drug Abuse and his research is generally used by law enforcement and marijuana opponents.

Note: In the interest of full disclosure, The State of California says marijuana smoke *causes* cancer:

The Office of Environmental Health Hazard Assessment (OEHHA) of the California Environmental Protection Agency has added marijuana smoke to the Proposition 65 list effective June 19, 2009 as known to the State Of California to cause cancer, according to the OEHHA website.

Vaporizing Marijuana: An Alternative to Smoking Joints, Bongs & Blunts

Vaporizing cannabis instead of smoking it can help reduce the potential of harm to the body because vaporizing marijuana activates the medicinal cannabinoids without actually burning the plant matter. Dr. Tod H. Mikuriya says, "The usual irritating and toxic breakdown products of burning utilized with smoking are totally avoided with vaporization".

If you don't have a vaporizer, baking marijuana at 150 degrees C (302 degrees F) for five minutes will kill microorganisms, especially molds without degrading the THC. (Levitz & Diamond 1991)

Additional ways to use medical marijuana:

- Pill & Capsule

- Inhaler

- Topical Oil

- Drinking

- Cannabis edibles

- Transdermal Patch

- Intravenous Injection

- Suppositories

Ganja Millionaire Spotlight 8: Idrasil

Rationale: The 65-and-older age group is projected to grow 36% by 2020 compared to just 9% growth rate for the general population making hospice care among the fastest growing segments of healthcare.

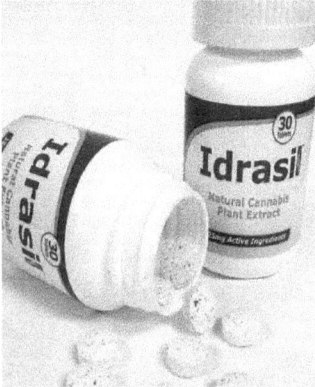

In hospitals, nursing homes and for caregivers, smoked marijuana is not a practical means of administration for patients. A smokeless, natural pill that delivers all the medicinal benefits of raw marijuana has tremendous potential, including use as a once-a-day type dietary supplement.

Idrasil is the new, new thing released May 2012 and boosts some impressive benefits:

- Idrasil is whole, natural THC, CBD & CBN extracted from the plant (aka whole plant extract)

- Idrasil contains all 3 major cannabinoids (THC, CBD, &CBN) in combination with 66 other natural cannabinoids.

- Idrasil patients report efficacy with whole, natural THC, CBD & CBN orally ingested

- Idrasil's proprietary technology isolates all cannabinoids from the plant offering a *"pure extraction"* without the use of oils or other additives

- Idrasil allows the caregiver to provide a consistent formula and measurable dosage every time.

Advantages of Idrasil

* No smoking

* Standardized dosage, 25mg tablets

* Lab tested - Bacteria free

* No sugar or salt

* Non addictive

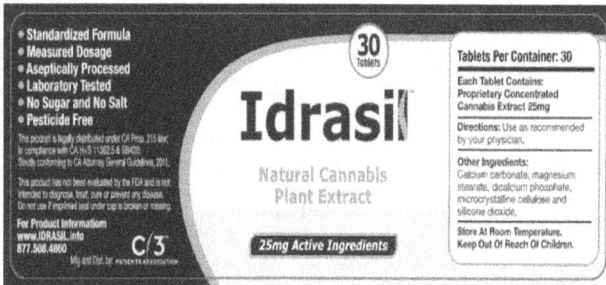

Idrasil is reimbursable by most insurance plans according to Idrasil website and its' patent is valid until 2037. Idrasil is marketed in conjunction with Doobons in California. Should real-world use of this product confirm the company's claims, the potential of this product and products like it are noteworthy.

XII. UFO's & Weed: Out of the Closet of Government Secrecy

Many believe the U.S. government knows more about controversial matters such as weed and ufo's etc. than is told. Most Americans understand that government secrecy, when in the interest of national security, is proper and necessary.

The 9/11 Commission concluded in its report that *too much* secrecy can put our nation at risk by hindering accountability, oversight and information sharing. This is according to John Podesta of the Center for American Progress testifying before the Senate Judiciary Committee on the Constitution in 2008.

Mr. Podesta added that excessive secrecy slows the development of scientific and technical knowledge and short circuits public debate, eroding confidence in government actions and causes people to second-guess legitimate restrictions.

While the 9/11 Commission and Senate Judiciary Committee's discussions were not specifically about cannabis, it begs the question...is there something about marijuana that we are not being told. If the primary danger of marijuana to a patient is the act of smoking it versus other methods of ingestion, wouldn't it have been labeled with warnings like tobacco and legalized a long time ago?

Ganja Millionaire Spotlight 9: City of Oakland

Rationale: This beautiful city in the San Francisco Bay Area, led by a creative city council, has been at the forefront of the medical marijuana movement in the United States.

Like many cities in the U.S., Oakland, California is no stranger to illegal drugs, drug use, addiction and the associated ills caused by drugs. A heroin epidemic ravaged the city in the 60's. More recently, a crack cocaine epidemic in the 1990's had catastrophic effects on families and the community. Crack cocaine altered daily life in Oakland and led to mass incarceration, broken spirits and dreams never realized. Crime went up, especially gun violence and murders. Children, many born addicted, grew up hungry and without the guidance of parents who were drug addicts and/or in prison because of drugs. Many did not survive this hurricane. Oakland had never witnessed the depravity caused by crack cocaine and is still healing from it.

Yet marijuana had always been there; viewed perhaps by some as a nuisance or a curiosity, but nothing more. Reasonable minds can distinguish between a *'hard drug'* like crack and a *'soft drug'* such as marijuana. The citizens of Oakland and the city leaders, making that distinction, approved a measure that would become a frontrunner of medical marijuana initiatives.

Proposition 215, also known as Compassionate Use Act of 1996, is a voter-approved initiative allowing for state authorized medical marijuana in California

Measure Z, a voter-approved initiative passed November 2, 2004, placed *cannabis possession* in the *lowest law enforcement priority* category in the City of Oakland and established one of the nation's first medical marijuana programs.

Taxing Weed

Oakland, California also took the progressive action of establishing the first business tax ever on retail marijuana sales in the U.S. The tax, which took effect January 1, 2010, was approved by approx. 80 percent of voters in 2008 and imposes an additional tax for "cannabis businesses".

Trial by Fire

In 2010, Oakland City Council became the first in California to support a marijuana legalization measure. The City Attorney at that time, John Russo, was also on record in support of ending the prohibition on marijuana.

Oakland has served as a model to the nation in providing safe access to medical marijuana but has come under federal scrutiny. Several dispensaries have been closed after recent raids. Oakland's new City Attorney, Barbara Parker, is concerned about Californians being deprived this "vital medicine". She is a former Assistant U.S. Attorney for the Northern District.

Honorable Mention: Denver, Colorado

Honorable Mention: Seattle, Washington

Ganja Millionaire Spotlight 10: Bhang Chocolate

Rationale: A tasty medicinal treat without smoking.

Bhang, the Original Cannabis Chocolate, using premium ingredients and gourmet technique, delivers a consistent, potent, and safe line of medicinal products.

Looking for the nearest dispensary that sells Bhang? At press time, Bhang's website is almost finished and will have a great locator map. In the meantime, you can send them your zip code and they will send you some suggestions. Website: bhangchocolate.com

XIII. U.S. Drug Enforcement Administration (DEA)

"Smoked marijuana has not withstood the rigors of science - it is not medicine and it is not safe." DEA official position on smoking marijuana

"The evidence in this record clearly shows that marijuana has been accepted as capable of relieving the distress of great numbers of very ill people, and doing so with safety under medical supervision. It would be unreasonable, arbitrary and capricious for DEA to continue to stand between those sufferers and the benefits of this substance in light of the evidence in this record. - DEA Administrative Law Judge, Administrative ruling on Petition to Reschedule Marijuana Sept. 6, 1988

What They Do

While individual voices within DEA may differ from the agency's official position, anyone interested in the industrial hemp and medical marijuana industries should understand DEA and its role in federal drug law enforcement.

The Drug Enforcement Administration (DEA) is a world class, heavily tasked federal enforcement agency under the U.S. Dept. of Justice charged with combating international drug trafficking, domestic drug enforcement of the Controlled Substances Act, classifying drugs and approving drug registrations. DEA also has sole responsibility for coordinating and pursuing U.S. drug investigations abroad.

Special Agents

Over half of DEA's more than 10,000 agents have the highly coveted Special Agent designation. Special agents undergo additional training, psychological and background screening, which can include a polygraph test.

The 420 Exception

DEA Special Agents can have no history of drug use. The only exception to this hard and fast rule is "youthful experimentation" with you guessed it, marijuana!

DEA Has Oversight of State Medical Marijuana Programs

The message on the flag in the photo on the left suggests a lack of understanding and is counter-productive. In a nutshell, the *U.S. Supreme Court* has ruled DEA has oversight of state medical marijuana programs. U.S. v. Oakland Cannabis Buyers Cooperatives (2001) and Gonzales v. Raich (2005)

Controlled Substances Act (1970)

The Controlled Substances Act, enacted as Title II of the Comprehensive Drug Abuse Prevention and Control Act of 1970, replaced the Marijuana Tax Act of 1937 after it was found unconstitutional in 1969 by the U.S. Supreme Court in the case of *Leary v. United States*, 395 U.S. 6

The Controlled Substances Act created five 'schedules' with varying qualifications for each substance. Schedule I is the most restrictive schedule and Schedule V is the least restrictive. Dept. of Health & Human Services (DHHS), DEA and FDA determine which drugs are added, transferred within or removed from the schedule.

Schedule I criteria:

- drug has high potential for abuse,

- drug has no currently accepted medical use in treatment in U.S.

- drug has lack of accepted safe use of the drug.

Includes: GHB, Marijuana, Heroin, MDMA (Ecstasy), Peyote, Mescaline

Schedule II criteria:

- drug has a high potential for abuse,

- drug has a currently accepted medical use in treatment in U.S.

- drug may lead to severe psychological and physical dependence

Includes: Cocaine, Opium, Morphine, Methamphetamine, Pure Codeine

Schedule III

- drug potential for abuse less than schedule I and II drugs

- drug has a currently accepted medical use in treatment in U.S.

- drug may lead to low or moderate physical dependence or high psychological dependence

Includes: Anabolic steroids, Barbiturates, Marinol

Schedule IV includes cough suppressants including "syrup" (promethazine codeine), diazepam (Valium) and Alprazolam (Xanax). These drugs

Schedule V includes certain opium and codeine preparations and is the least restrictive schedule.

Shafer Commission

The Comprehensive Drug Abuse Prevention and Control Act of 1970 also established the National Commission on Marijuana and Drug Abuse to study marijuana abuse in the U.S. The Commission, also known as the Shafer Commission after its chairman Raymond Shafer, recommended decriminalizing marijuana in small quantities. During the Commission's First Report to Congress, Mr. Shafer stated:

The criminal law is too harsh a tool to apply to personal possession even in the effort to discourage use. It implies an overwhelming indictment of the behavior which we believe is not appropriate. The actual and potential harm of use of the drug is not great enough to justify intrusion by the criminal law into private behavior, a step which our society takes only with the greatest reluctance.

Rescheduling Marijuana

Marijuana is listed in Schedule I as having no medical value which prevents research and patient access to this drug. In light of the medical research and DHHS's patent on cannabinoids, marijuana advocates, including state attorney's general have petitioned DEA to reschedule marijuana into Schedule II or III.

XIV. More Industry Watchdogs: The Power Players

Office of National Drug Control Policy (ONDCP) - a branch of the Executive Office of the President and advises the President on drug policy. ONDCP acknowledges "THC, the primary active chemical in marijuana, can be useful for treating some medical problems" but is not fond of smoked marijuana as a means of delivery.

National Institute of Drug Abuse (NIDA) - NIDA is a U.S. federal research institute that funds marijuana research and administers the Univ. of Mississippi federal contract to grow medical cannabis for research and study.

Dept. of Health and Human Services (DHHS) - Makes the medical and scientific determinations concerning drug scheduling. If DHHS determines marijuana has accepted medical value, it will be removed from the most restrictive Schedule I. Also holds the Cannabinoids patent.

Food & Drug Administration (FDA) - Though FDA has not yet recognized the medicinal value of cannabis nor has it approved smoked cannabis for any condition, it has approved several cannabinoids for medical therapies, including dronabinol (Marinol), Naboline and Canasol. FDA also approves the medical marijuana distributed in the Compassionate IND program.

World Health Organization (WHO) - "While THC has long been known to reduce the increased intraocular pressure of glaucoma, it has not been fully studied therapeutically...Therapeutic uses of cannabinoids are being demonstrated by controlled studies in the treatment of glaucoma". - *Cannabis: A Health Perspective and Research Agenda (1997) report by World Health Organization*

United Nations Commission on Narcotic Drugs - can also add or transfer a drug to or from one of the Schedules.

Ganja Millionaire Spotlight 11: Portugal

Rationale: One country's innovative approach to addressing drug use and its associated social and health issues is effective. "The changes that were made in Portugal provide an interesting before-and-after study on the possible effects of decriminalization," says the European Monitoring Centre for Drugs and Drug Addiction.

Portugal, in 2001, became the first country in the world to decriminalize all drugs.

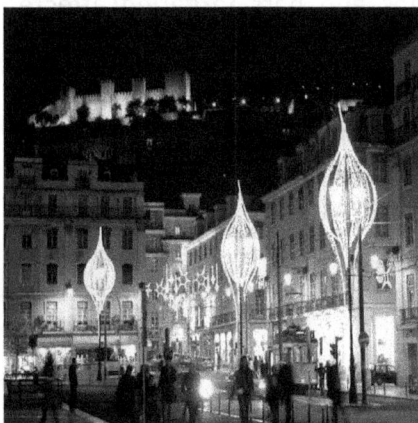

Portugal's Problems

- In 1997, IV drug users represented 45 % of AIDS cases in Portugal

- Portugal had the highest rate of HIV among IV drug users in the European Union in 1999, thus targeting drug usage was seen also as part of HIV prevention.

- In the 1990's Portugal had 100,000 "problematic" drug users, a high number for such a small country and by the end of the 90's, the number of heroin users was between 50,000 and 100,000.

Portugal's Solutions

Enter The National Strategy for the Fight against Drugs in 1999 to combat these problems. To say that Portugal simply decriminalized drugs as a response to drug related ills oversimplifies the bold, creative, comprehensive actions Portugal deployed:

Expanded harm reduction efforts

1) Needle Exchange Program - drug users can exchange used syringes at pharmacies across the country. The kit contains clean needle syringes, a condom, rubbing alcohol and a written message promoting AIDS prevention and addiction treatment

2) Street Teams - promotes safe injection practices and supplies needles and injecting equipment on the street. Many street teams are still running today.

3) Media Campaign - promotes awareness of drug addiction and HIV transmission via needle sharing thru TV, radio, press, and posters placed in clubs and bars targeting affected segments of Portugal's' population

4) Doubled public fund investment - (drug treatment and prevention services) - provided for more detoxification units, public outpatient facilities, day centers and specialized treatment facilities, both public and private. Investment also included substitution treatment, after-care and social re-integration and a system to monitor drug treatment being developed.

Shift in Drug Policy

Portugal's new drug reforms included a shift in the way drug addiction was viewed and defined and in the way drug users were dealt with when caught with drugs. Instead of tightening drug laws, Portugal relaxed them, believing change and innovation was necessary.

"Drug addiction is a disease" said Dr. Joao Goulao, president of the Institute of Drugs and Drug Addiction and one of the chief architects of Portugal's drug reforms, set in place in 2000 and legally effective July 2001. "When you are sick, you must be faced like a patient and treated like that," Dr. Goulao added.

If an individual is found with a small amount of drugs, the drugs are confiscated and she is issued a summons to appear before a Dissuasion Committee panel that strongly recommends treatment over fines and/or incarceration. The Committee can also impose a broad range of sanctions on the offender.

To be clear, drugs are still illegal in Portugal, in compliance with international treaties and conventions, and criminal penalties remain on the books for dealers, illegal growers and traffickers.

Portugal's' Results

One critic of Portugal's new drug law reforms says drug consumption overall in has risen 4.2 percent since 2001 and that decriminalization benefits are being over hyped. However a study by the Cato Institute of Portugal's reforms and other statistical data suggests otherwise:

- Drug crime is down
- More addicts are seeking treatment,
- HIV diagnoses are down by 17% among drug users
- Infection rates and deaths associated with drug use have fallen,
- Illegal drug use by teens declined, especially among 15-19 year olds

The prediction that Portugal would become a haven for drug use did not come true. To the contrary, "There is no doubt that the phenomenon of addiction is in decline in Portugal," confirms Dr. Goulao.

🍁 Ganja Millionaire Spotlight 12: Manitoba Harvest

Rationale: Manitoba Harvest, maker of quality consumer hemp products and was instrumental in Canada's progressive hemp movement.

Officially founded in 1998, Manitoba Harvest Hemp Foods & Oils actually started much earlier. Company co-founders aligned with farmers and academics in the early 1990's to create the Manitoba Hemp Alliance. In 1995, the Alliance successfully secured government permission and funding to plant hemp trials. The experimental trials helped alleviate misconceptions regarding industrial hemp, gained government support, and caught the interest of the trade. Manitoba Harvest was born immediately after industrial hemp was legalized.

The company started small focusing on manufacturing the highest quality hemp food products while educating people on the nutritional benefits of hemp foods. Manitoba Harvest also partners direct with hemp farmers to source the raw, non-genetically modified hemp seed. The company controls every aspect of the production process and holds itself to the highest operational standards. Products are made fresh in-house, a state-of-the-art kosher and organic certified facility. Manitoba Harvest also goes through voluntary audits and certifications to ensure quality.

Manitoba Harvest is based in Winnipeg, Manitoba, Canada and serves North America, Europe and Asia.

No Patient Denied Foundation

Fifty United Medical Marijuana States

Half a million cancer patients are dying due to a shortage of cancer drugs every year in the United States. Additionally, many patients who may benefit from medical marijuana for a variety of illnesses do not have access to the drug because of where they live.

No Patient Denied, a recently formed non-profit organization, believes no qualifying patient should be denied the medicinal benefit of marijuana for approved ailments. Fully appreciating medical marijuana initiatives are generally voter-approved, No Patient Denied was created to promote education and awareness in non-medical marijuana states with upcoming or pending state medical marijuana initiatives on the ballot about the importance of patient access for all Americans.

Authors Note: Interim Executive Director is needed to help build and grow this organization. Bay Area resident preferred

XV. United States Office of Cannabis (U.S.O.C.)
aka U.S. Cannabis Office (a model for success) by Kenwa Jabuki

OCDETF certified, independent federal agency, or fully funded operational division of DEA, headed up by the 'Commander' assisted by an Executive Officer. USOC would maintain offices, the Hemptagon (just kidding), in Washington D.C. and Oakland, California. USOC reports to DEA and ONDCP. USOC would operate with respect to and in accordance with all federal drug laws, relevant international treaties and conventions.

This agency specifically oversees city, county and/or state medical marijuana and industrial hemp programs. It will also serve as a clearinghouse, consolidating information regarding hemp production and medical marijuana from all participating U.S. states. As the U.S. cannabis industry evolves, having this information centralized will assist USOC and partner agencies in keeping up with the growth of the industry and continued enforcement of U.S. drug laws at the local, state and federal levels, command and control.

USOC will establish an Advisory Council which includes a representative from ONDCP, DEA, DHHS, FDA, USDA, Institute of Medicine, American Medical Association, American College of Physicians and NIDA. Any member of the Advisory Council can make recommendations for consideration and possible adoption as an objective, operational modality or policy. USOC publish a quarterly report.

USOC Website

Each hemp producing and medical marijuana city, county or state must create and maintain a page on the USOC website providing their specific registration requirements for program participation, applicable laws, limits, rules, regulations and any additional information. Each public entity is responsible for maintaining the accuracy of the information on their respective state page. USOC also provides information to assist all those participating in the programs.

USOC general counsel handles legal issues and matters arising from violations. Counsel can archive and make available via the website, all federal drug laws that are still good law as well as past, current and pending hemp and marijuana legislation and case law etc.

Medicinal Marijuana Division

Director of this division reports directly to the Commander. This division has oversight over all state medical marijuana programs. To keep agency funding substantially budget neutral, a $50 registration fee will be assessed to every doctor per patient they approve for a medical marijuana recommendation. Recommendations must be renewed annually. This fee will most likely be passed on to the individual medical marijuana patient which should not be a hindrance to patient accessibility as the price for a medical marijuana evaluation has already decreased from around $150 to $50-75 as more doctors are providing evaluations, thus driving the price down. A copy of every doctor patient recommendation must be on file with USOC. Every doctor that performs medical marijuana evaluations must fill out a brief registration form on the U.S.O.C. website, upload recommendations at time of issue.

Hemp Division

Director of this division reports directly to the Commander. This division is charged with overseeing the U.S. industrial hemp industry which is currently non-existent. The Hemp Division maintains shared oversight of state run industrial hemp agriculture programs with USDA, and support hemp farmers in the program via information, marketing support, equipment grants, etc. Also works closely with state agriculture agencies and USDA.

Reviving hemp production, will enable U.S. hemp products that are not labor intensive can be made as cost effectively as can be made abroad with comparable profitability.

Hemp farmers are assessed an annual $3900 registration fee for a hemp production registration license. Fee is paid directly to USOC and is in addition to any state level assessment. The hemp farmer fee is also independent of any fee due U.S.D.A. who would have shared oversight over all U.S. hemp farmers and production.

Farmers must use certified hemp seeds and is accountable if marijuana is grown within the hemp field, subject to fine and/or imprisonment. USOC officers would conduct random inspections of farms handled by USOC and take samples from plants for chemical analysis to ensure only hemp and not marijuana is grown.

Research Division

Research Division Director reports directly to the Commander. This division is staffed by fifty doctors, scientists and research analysts. Among other things, USOC research team will analyze samples taken from hemp farms to make sure female cannabis plants (marijuana) are not being grown on hemp farms. Industrial hemp is the male cannabis plant. Research may also conduct independent cannabis research and possibly fund research projects for medical centers, universities, conduct studies, surveys, patent work etc.

There is currently hundreds of different strains (varieties) of hemp and marijuana, resulting in different growth characteristics, yields, quality of fiber. Some strains are more resistant to mold, mildew, pest and disease. In the case of medicinal marijuana, different strains provide different and/or additional medical benefit and different side effects (psychoactive effects), due to varying levels of THC, CBD and CBN's.

Consequently, to protect national interest in this medicinal and industrial plant and to aid in continued research of cannabis, USOC will immediately commence building a **Seed Vault** containing every strain of cannabis (hemp & marijuana) known to man and those to be developed, as hybrid strains are being created regularly. The bulk of these seeds would be preserved for long-term storage with some being used for R&D.

Compliance & Enforcement Division

To give the agency teeth, USOC would maintain a modest compliance and enforcement division of 50 - 100 men and women. These officers perform random inspections of hemp farms and medical marijuana dispensaries and collectives and carry out additional agency duties. Also works with other agencies in this regard such as DEA, IRS etc.

Command & Control

As the American public gains knowledge of the benefits of hemp and medical marijuana, states are likely to see more ballot initiatives to establish hemp & medical marijuana programs. At that point, the federal government can either usurp the will of the people in those states or take a more proactive approach.

Establishing an agency substantively similar to USOC model while the U.S. hemp and medical marijuana industries are nil and early stage in most states will provide for more effective control than trying to cage a behemoth.

Note: A similar USOC type agency could be duplicated in other nations amenable to easing restriction concerning the cannabis component of the international drug treaties.

Hemp Hummers

For transportation, USOC could drive surplus military vehicles equipped to run on gas, hemp fuel, natural gas, methanol etc. in addition to brand new, high performance enforcement vehicles.

U.S. Federal Marijuana Tax Act of 2013 *(proposed)* - 3% federal tax on all medical marijuana sales and an 8% tax for hemp farmers. This revenue could be utilized to fund drug addiction awareness and treatment, continued cannabis research and research grants, tax incentives and equipment grants for farmers, builders who use hemp products etc., law enforcement, operational/administrative costs and the *Cannabis Border Alliance Program.*

U.S. Cannabis Museum - located in Washington D.C. with funding coming from individuals, corporations, endowments, grants and foundations an. The building could be designed and built by Push Design, maker of the Hemp House in Asheville, North Carolina and its team of volunteers. Construction of the museum would include hemp, natural fibers, recycled materials i.e. wood & metals etc. The museum will highlight the history of cannabis throughout the world and specifically the United States. The museum will display relevant pictures, posters, paintings, videos and include historical items like Henry Ford's Hemp Car, and vehicles that incorporate hemp composite parts such as Lotus, Kestrel, BMW, and Mercedes. The museum will house reduced size scale models of the Hemp Houses in N.C. and the UK, Hemcrete blocks, ancient hemp collectibles and more. The museum could be located in a state with historical ties to hemp production like Kentucky, Pennsylvania, Missouri, Wisconsin etc. but I believe hemp and its ties to the founding fathers are much stronger and overriding, hence D.C. first option.

XVI. The Benefits of State Medical Marijuana Programs

There benefit of state medical marijuana programs:

- Allows for better command and control of illicit drug trade and use - all patients must be registered.

- Provides safe access to medical marijuana to cannabis patients with a doctor's recommendation.

- Helps reduce illicit drug trade by reducing U.S. demand for and dependence on marijuana coming from outside the U.S.

- Reduces street crime, street level drug sales, assaults and robberies, putting a significant dent in the street dealers business and thus increasing public safety.

- Frees up law enforcement to address the more serious issue of violent crime

- Removes drug dealing from the street in public view

- Can provide much needed revenue to municipalities and the city, county, state and federal levels.

- Increases health & wellness as many dispensaries and collectives test the cannabis for harmful pesticides, fungi, bacteria etc.

- Restores the dignity of the cannabis patient

XVII. Predictions for the Growth of Medical Marijuana

The medical marijuana industry is further along the road towards legitimacy than it was even five years ago. However, regulatory uncertainty should be a consideration because though medicinal cannabis is allowed in 17 states and D.C., it is still illegal federally and thus there have continued to be DEA raids on dispensaries and growers that violate federal law.

With that said, opportunities continue to exist for those willing learn the ins and outs of the industry and respect the fact that the DEA has and will continue to have ultimate oversight.

Medical marijuana represents a $1.7 billion in annual revenue year rivaling Pfizer's Viagra with $1.9 billion in annual sales according to See Change Strategy, a financial analysis firm specializing in new markets. The industry is expected to double in the next five years in the 16 states where medical cannabis is voter approved and should 20 more states pass similar laws, annual revenue could grow to $8.9 billion by 2016.

Public Opinion Shifting Towards Medical Marijuana Legalization

The increase in annual medical marijuana revenue coincides with a historic shift in public attitude towards medical marijuana. For the first time ever, Gallop reports that 50% of Americans now favor the use of marijuana for medical reasons and 70% favor making it legal for doctors to prescribe it for medical purposes. Public opinion should continue to increase as awareness of the benefits of industrial hemp and marijuana spreads.

Support for Making Use of Marijuana Legal

Do you think the use of marijuana should be made legal, or not?

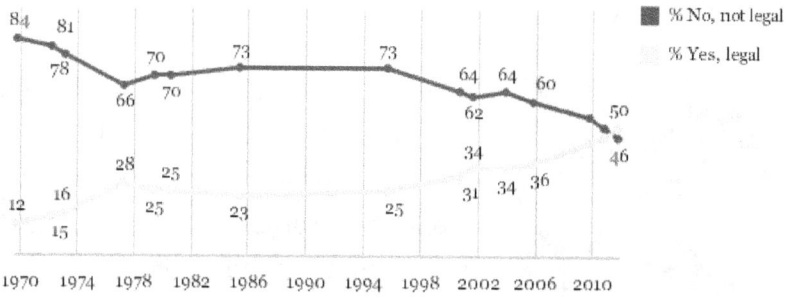

GALLUP

- California and Colorado currently make up most of the wholesale and retail sales nationwide with 92 percent share. This will change as more states implement medical marijuana programs that allow for dispensaries.
- The number of potential consumers for medical marijuana in U.S. currently is around 24.8 million. This reflects the number of Americans with qualifying ailments living in a current "legal" state. There are at present fewer than 800,000 patients in these states.
- Washington, Arizona and Michigan are considered well-positioned for significant growth.

I believe many well-known, respected brand name companies in addition to Scotts Miracle-Gro have an interest in the medical marijuana market but need to see the industry stabilize before risking brand equity.

In Closing

A Plant of Renown

Our ancient ancestors, founding fathers, modern doctors and now the U.S. government have all tapped the benefits of cannabis. Marijuana is the only plant on Earth that has the medicinal compounds that rightly qualify it to be called *medical marijuana* and *medicine*. No other plant in the world has as many industrial and medicinal applications and no other plant has been more maligned or as hotly debated.

While it is doubtful the government is going to interrupt the nightly news to announce that marijuana has medical value, it is the hope of millions that this position is evolving.

Shifting International Drug Policy

There is general agreement among many that the war on drugs has failed and specifically that global prohibition on marijuana was ill-founded. City councils, mayors, state panels, governors and even Heads of State are talking about improving the drug policy.

Control

Policy shift would help reduce the flow of illicit drug trade, abuse and addiction

Financial

Revenue generated by medical marijuana programs and hemp production could help economies.

Civil Liberties

Does the cannabis prohibition violate free speech? A question raised by the DHHS Secretary during the international drug convention in the 1920's.

Does prohibition violate an individual's right to bodily privacy?

Ethical

Is it ethical to reschedule synthetic THC into less restrictive schedules while marijuana, the source of natural THC, remains in Schedule I?

The ethics of a patent on cannabinoids showing marijuana has medical value but officially maintaining marijuana has no value?

Moral & Humanitarian

To my mind, this is the most important reason to ease the restriction on cannabis and where world leaders can come out smelling like roses. There are a lot of Aunt Elouise's and Uncle Earl's out there staring at the T.V. screen, suffering from various medical conditions, worthy of a quality of life lived with dignity. Let no patient be denied.

Amending the treaties and convention's to allow for state-authorized medical marijuana programs and industrial hemp production would put to rest recurring civil liberty and ethical questions raised and make drug policy more effective.

Ganja Millionaires Needed

I hope everyone who reads this book is enriched in the knowledge of cannabis and the dynamics surrounding it. Some of you have read this book because of a deeper interest and perhaps an idea. Your idea may provide a treatment or a cure, preserve and sustain our planet, provide jobs and opportunities, revolutionize a process or improve happiness and quality of life. The light is on the horizon and as the industrial hemp and medical marijuana industries continue to grow worldwide, so will opportunities to become the next Ganja Millionaire!

Peace & Buds,

Kenwa Jabuki

15 Hemp Businesses You Can Start for Under $100

Ganja Millionaire Opportunities on a Shoestring!

Since ancient times, hemp has been associated with life, friendship, purity and protection from evil. Hemp products are hip, funky, eternally trendy and eco-friendly. Equally exciting is the fact that hemp products are healthy, good for the hair, body and more. These benefits, coupled with a low cost of entry make hemp businesses excellent income opportunities. I did some brainstorming and came up with as many hemp money makers I could think of that you can start for under $100. The ability to start and operate them from your home, kitchen, workshop, garage etc. was also a criterion to make the list. You can buy the supplies you will need to get started locally and when necessary, order them online. If you earn just an extra $100-200 a week with your new hemp business, at the end of the month you'll find that buys a lot of groceries and pays some bills. Begin with one or several of the following ideas and grow your hemp business from there. Best wishes for your success!

Hemp Business 1: Hemp Soap

Cosmetics made with organic botanicals and natural extracts are increasing in popularity. Hemp soap is great for the skin and very effective! Another good thing about hemp soap is the low cost to your customers and that it can generate repeat business for you. You have two options in starting a hemp soap business. You can buy premade hemp soap wholesale or make

your own right from your kitchen, saving yourself the shipping costs. There are plenty of homemade soap recipes and *'how to make hemp soap'* videos online to help you get going without spending a lot of money.

As you will learn, there are many recipes and ways to make hemp soap. Choose your own color or colors for your soap, extra ingredients such as oats etc. or create swirl designs, tri-color layers and even stamp the name of your hemp soap or business on the bars you make if branding is also a goal.

You may branch out and make and/or offer lavender, orange peel, lemongrass soaps etc. Sky's the limit! Don't waste any time second-guessing yourself. The investment is nominal so your risk is extremely low.

Hemp Business 2: Hemp Scented Oils

According to Chemist's Corner, Fine fragrances make up about 10% of the cosmetic industry and represent the highest profit segment of the industry.

Hemp fragrance oils can be layered with perfume or cologne or worn alone as an alternative. By making your own hemp scented oils, you can develop your own exclusive fragrances.

Of course, the base oil you will use for your hemp fragrance oil line will be chiefly hemp essential oils which you can buy in the industrial gallon size and larger (Bulk Virgin Hemp Seed Oil). However you can also add grape seed oil (antioxidant) and arnica oil (aches & pains). You can find these oils at your local health foods store.

Less expensive oils include vegetable oils such as safflower, rice bran (antioxidant-makes skin glow), sesame oil, soybean oil, canola oil, peanut oil, sweet almond oil. You can find these oils at your local grocery store and/or health food store. Color your oils to signify different scents if you'd like.

Search: *how to make homemade scented oils, how to make homemade scented oils videos*

Hemp Business 3: Hemp Bracelets & Necklaces

Hemp jewelry is funky, stylish and inexpensive. You can buy premade hemp bracelets or make your own. Hemp twine is available at your local crafts or beads supply or hardware store.

There are many different colors of hemp twine available. You can add beads, rocks, crystals, designs, etc. to jazz up your product line. Google *hemp bracelets images* and you'll get plenty of ideas.

You can find wholesalers and supplies by searching: *hemp bracelets wholesale & hemp bracelet supplies.*

Hemp Business 4: Hemp Lip Balm & Hemp Lip Gloss

You can pack your lip balm in tubes with your own private label or pack your balms in custom tins. Sell your hemp balms to friends and family, on websites, stores and more.

If you're planning to sell your lip balm, FDA has some guidelines for you when creating the labeling and packaging.

FDA's Cosmetics Labeling Guide: http://www.fda.gov/cosmetics/cosmeticlab elinglabelclaims/cosmeticlabelingmanual/uc m126444.htm

Search: How to Make Hemp Lip Balm, How to Make Lip Balm etc.

Hemp Business 5: Hemp Bikinis

This hemp business doesn't require much fabric per bikini but allows for a decent retail price for your time and effort. Hemp bikinis retail for $80 to over $130 per unit. For those not interested in making your own custom bikinis, consider buying them wholesale.

Search: *hemp fabrics, hemp bikinis, how to make bikinis*

Hemp Business 6: Hemp Mini Dolls

Dolls are timeless gifts. Very little is needed, in terms of materials, to make these products which great year-round for birthdays, holidays etc. Start off making *'mini'* dolls so you can make, and thus sell more, for your money. Here's a sample of what you will need.

Mini Doll Making

For *'How to'* instructions, search: *how to make mini dolls, how to make mini dolls videos* and you'll be off to a running start.

Hemp Business 7: Hemp Herbal Hair Care Products

Approximately 20% of all cosmetic products sold are hair products. Shampoos and conditioners make up most of this market since almost everyone uses shampoo.

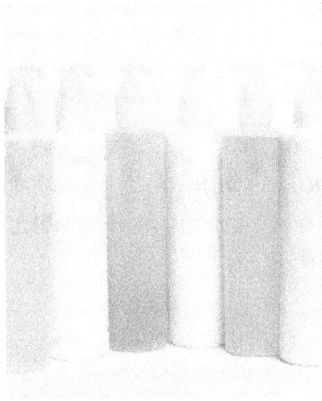

The ancient Chinese used hemp to prevent hair loss and grey hair. Organic Hemp oil hair care products could represent the next generation of natural, healthy hair management essentials. Make hemp shampoo and conditioner.

Search:

How to make hemp shampoo,

How to make hair shampoo and conditioner

Herbal hemp shampoo recipe

Hemp Business 8: Hemp Skin Care Products

Hemp seed oil is excellent for skin care products because of its regenerative properties. Make hemp lotion, facial and body creams and shaving products.

Hemp skin care, when applied topically, nourishes the skin and has anti-inflammatory effects.

You can sell your hemp skin care line locally, on websites, friends, family, stores etc.!

If you're planning on selling your hemp skin care, FDA has some guidelines for you when creating the labeling and packaging.

FDA's Cosmetics Labeling Guide:

http://www.fda.gov/cosmetics/cosmeticlabelinglabelclaims/cosmeticlabelingmanual/ucm126444.htm

Search:

How to make lotion

How to make your organic skin care products

How to make hemp oil skin care

How to Make Hemp Oil Aloe Vera Facial Moisturizer,

- *Establishing Your Own In-Home Business Making Skin Care Products*

Hemp Business 9: Nail Polish

While this isn't exactly a hemp business, it is an income opportunity that doesn't take a lot of cash to launch. All you need to make your own nail polish is clear nail polish, eye shadow (color of your choice) and nail polish remover.

Create your own exclusive colors, add glitter etc.

Search:

How to make nail polish

Hemp Business 10: Hemp Shoes & Socks

Hemp socks are a low cost way to get started making some money while investing a minimal amount of cash.

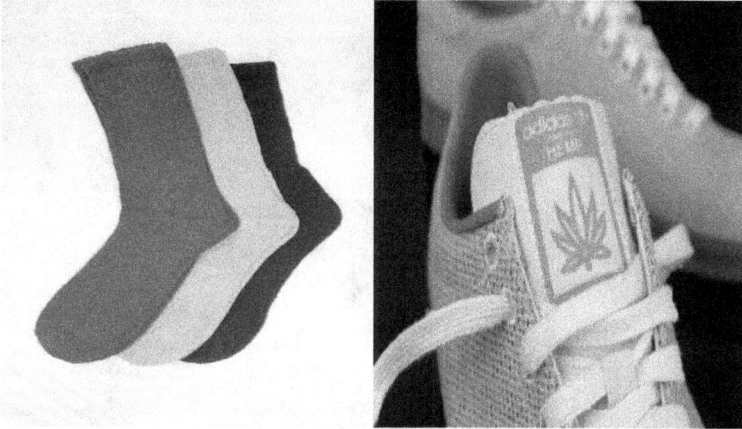

Search: *hemp socks* and *hemp shoes*

Hemp Business 11: Hemp Clothing

This is a hemp business with exciting prospects. Ideally, it's best to really have a budget before launching a full blown hemp apparel business. If you do have money for inventory however, you'll find plenty of eye-catching hemp products you can offer. Hemp clothing is durable yet comfortable. Hemp blended apparel is generally a 55/45 cotton/hemp blend and there's also 100% hemp clothing available. Hemp apparel is available wholesale. Patagonia, Armani, Calvin Klein and Adidas and more have produced hemp products.

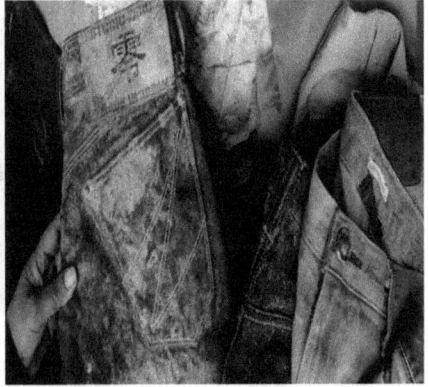

These Studio Zero hemp-stitched jeans survived the tsunami in Japan.

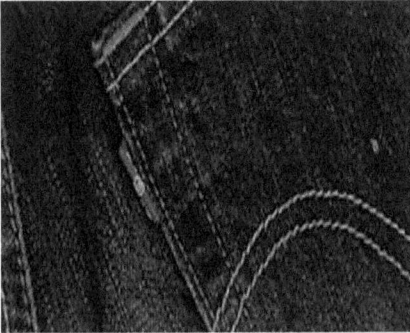

Levi's famed *Red Label* jeans were made of 40% hemp. The good ole days!

Search: *hemp apparel, hemp jeans* etc. and this will point you in the relevant direction.

Kenwa Jabuki

Hemp Business 12: Hemp Curtains

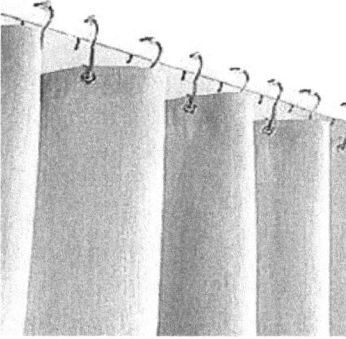

This is a very straightforward, simple hemp business. Get some hemp fabric, take your measurements, punch holes, insert eyelets and hangers. It's great if you can sew, however you can outsource the sewing or buy hemp curtains wholesale.

Search: *how to make hemp curtains, hemp curtains wholesale*

Hemp Business 13: Hemp Kitchen Towels

Search: *hemp kitchen towels, hemp fabrics, hemp textiles*

Hemp Business 14: Hemp Bedding & Linen

Your customers will sleep in comfort on hemp sheets and bedding.

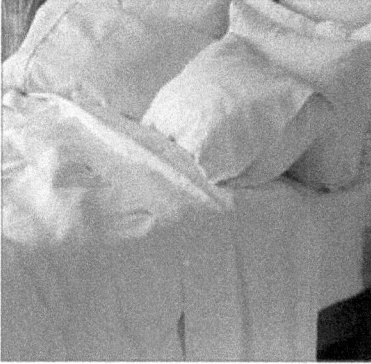

Search: *hemp textiles, hemp bedding, hemp linen*

Hemp Business 15: Hemp Bags & Laptop Covers

Hemp bags are available wholesale and for the industrious, you can make your own.

Sample bags from EarthDivas.com

Search: *hemp bags, how to make hemp bags, hemp bags wholesale etc.*

Hemp Business 16: Hemp Pillows

Hemp fabric, stuffing and a needle and thread is all you need to get going with your own hemp pillow business.

Search: *how to make hemp pillows, hemp pillows wholesale*

Additional ideas: Hemp Car Seat Covers & Hemp Handkerchiefs

XVIII. Jobs, Careers & Opportunities

Here are some current and future opportunities in the cannabis industries:

Hemp farmers and laborers

Hemp Industry suppliers

Hemp Processor

Hemp Apparel Designers

Hemp Apparel Manufacturers

Hemp Product & Apparel retailers

Bud-tenders

Medical Marijuana Delivery Service

Marketing

Accountants

Public Relations

Sales

Security

Receptionists

Administrative Assistants

Dispensary Management

Dispensary Owner

Marijuana Collective

Compliance Officer

Paralegals

Medical Marijuana Doctors

Medical Marijuana Lawyers

Tech Support

Patient Cultivators (Growers)

Dispensary Medical Marijuana Buyers

Edibles Chef's

Support Services i.e., massage, acupuncture, and grow classes

Law Enforcement

Research

Cultivator

Cannabis Cookbook

Hemp fabric & textiles

Hemp & Marijuana Beverages Waters & Soda

Medical Marijuana Evaluation Center

XIX. Countries Growing Industrial Hemp (as of April 20, 2012)

The United States is the only industrialized nation in the world that does not allow for hemp production. Below is a list of countries that are currently exploiting the benefits of hemp:

AUSTRALIA

Hemp research trials began in Tasmania in 1995. New South Wales also conducts research. Commercial production of hemp in Victoria has been ongoing since 1998. Queensland began production in 2002. Western Australia started licensing crops in 2004.

AUSTRIA

Hemp industry in Austria includes production of hem seed oil and medicines.

CANADA

Canada has licensed research crops since 1994. In addition to crops for fiber, one seed crop was licensed in 1995. More acres were planted in 1997. Licenses for commercial agriculture began in 1998.

A number of Canadian farmers are now growing organically-certified hemp crops yielding almost four million pounds per year.

CHILE

Chile has grown hemp in the recent past for seed oil production.

CHINA

For millennia, cannabis, both hemp and marijuana, has grown wild in China. China leads the world in hemp production and is the world's largest exporter of hemp & hemp textiles. The fabrics are of excellent quality. Medium dense fiber board is also available now. The Chinese word for hemp is "ma". Hemp has never been prohibited in China.

DENMARK

Denmark planted its first modern hemp trial crops in 1997. The country is committed to using organic growing methods.

FINLAND

Hemp has never been prohibited in Finland. In 1995 there was a resurgence of hemp with several small test plots. A seed variety for northern climates was developed called Finola, previously known by the breeder code "FIN-314". In 2003, Finola was accepted to the EU list of subsidized hemp cultivars. The Finnish word for hemp is "hennop".

FRANCE

France has never prohibited hemp production. France is a source of low-THC producing hemp for seed for other countries. France exports high quality hemp oil to the U.S. The French word for hemp is "hamppu".

GERMANY

Banned hemp in 1982 however research began again ten years later. In 1995, the ban on growing hemp was lifted and now many products and technologies are being developed. Food, clothes and paper are made from imported raw materials. Mercedes and BMW use hemp composite fibers in dashboards, door panels etc. The German word for hemp is "hanf".

GREAT BRITAIN

The U.K. lifted hemp prohibition in 1993. Animal bedding, paper and hemp textiles are being developed there. A government grant was given to develop new markets for natural fibers. Four thousand acres were grown in 1994. Subsidies of 230 British pounds per acre are given by the government to farmers for growing hemp.

HUNGARY

Hungary is currently rebuilding their hemp industry. Hungary is also one of the biggest exporters of hemp cordage, rugs and fabrics to the U.S. They also export hemp seed, paper and fiberboard. The Hungarian word for hemp is "kender".

INDIA

One of the world's largest producers of hemp and uses it for cordage, textiles and seeds. Hemp has never been prohibited in India.

ITALY

India has invested in the resurgence of hemp, especially for textile production. One thousand acres were planted for fiber in 2002. Giorgio Armani grows its own hemp for specialized textiles and has produced hemp jeans.

JAPAN

Custom requires that the Emperor and Shinto priests wear hemp garments in certain ceremonies in keeping with a rich tradition. Thus, there are small plots maintained for these purposes. Traditional spice mixes also include hemp seed. Japan supports a thriving retail market for a variety of hemp products.

NETHERLANDS

Conducted a four-year study to evaluate and test hemp for paper and developing specialized processing equipment. Some breeders are developing new strains of low-THC varieties. The Dutch word for hemp is "hennep".

NEW ZEALAND

New Zealand began hemp trials in 2001. Various cultivars are being planted in the northern and southern islands.

POLAND

Currently grows hemp for fabric and cordage and manufactures hemp particle board. Poland has used hemp to cleanse soils contaminated by heavy metals. The Polish word for hemp is "konopij".

ROMANIA

Romania is the largest commercial producer of hemp in Europe. Some Romanian hemp is exported to Hungary for processing and also exported to Western Europe and the U.S. The Romanian word for hemp is "cinepa".

RUSSIA

Russia maintains the largest hemp germplasm collection in the world at N.I. Vavilov Scientific Research Institute of St. Petersburg. The Russian word for hemp is "konoplya".

SLOVENIA

Grows hemp and manufactures currency paper with it.

SPAIN

Spain has never prohibited hemp. Spain produces hemp rope and textiles and exports hemp pulp for paper. The Spanish word for hemp is "canamo".

SWITZERLAND

Switzerland produces of hemp and hosts one of the largest hemp trade events in the world, Cannatrade.

TURKEY

Turkey has grown hemp for over 2,800 years for rope, caulking, birdseed, paper and fuel.

UKRAINE, EYGPT, KOREA, PORTUGAL AND THAILAND all produce hemp.

UNITED STATES

The United States is the world's largest importer of hemp. The U.S. granted the first hemp permit in over 40 years to Hawaii for an experimental quarter-acre plot in 1999. The license was renewed but the project has since been closed due to funding problems. Industrial hemp production is still prohibited in the United States.

Kenwa Jabuki

U.S. States with Pending Industrial Hemp Legislation (as of April 20, 2012)

KENTUCKY

HAWAII

VERMONT

NORTH DAKOTA

MONTANA

MINNESOTA

ILLINOIS

VIRGINIA

NEW MEXICO

ARKANSAS

MARYLAND

WEST VIRGINIA

MAINE

XX. U.S. Medical Marijuana States

Alaska

420 Law: Ballot Measure 8 (1998)

Plant Limit: 1 ounce usable, 6 plants [3 mature, 3 immature]

How to Register: Patients must obtain an identification card from the Alaska Bureau of Vital Statistics' Marijuana Registry. Application requires a fee of $25 and a signed statement from the patient's doctor that addresses the patient's condition, states that the doctor has personally examined the patient and details how the doctor came to the conclusion that medical marijuana was justified. Patients must have a "debilitating medical condition."

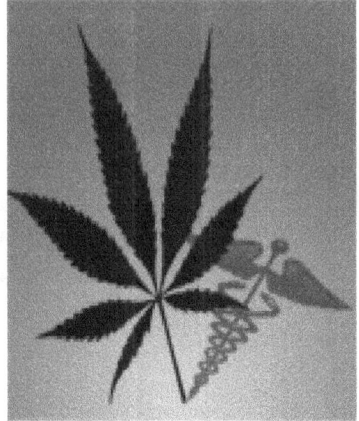

For More Info: Alaska Bureau of Vital Statistics – Marijuana Registry P.O. Box 110699 Juneau, AK 99811-0699 Phone: (907) 465-5423

Arizona

420 Law: Proposition 203 (2010)

Plant Limit: Up to 12 plants indoors [unless within 25 miles of a dispensary]

How to Register: Patients must obtain a valid doctor's recommendation for an approved medical condition which allows them to possess 2.5 ounces of cannabis or buy that much from a state approved dispensary in a 14-day period. The Arizona Dept. of

Health is still debating their final rules. In May 2012, Arizona began accepting applications to open dispensaries. They will accept 126 applications with final decisions coming in August 2012.

For More Info: Arizona Dept. of Health Services (ADHS) - Medical Marijuana Program 150 North 18th Avenue Phoenix, AZ 85007 (602) 542-1023

California

420 Law: Proposition 215 (1996)

Plant Limit: 8 ounces usable, 6 mature, 12 immature

How to Register: ID cards are not required. However they are recommended and can cost up to $75. To qualify for a cannabis card you must get a medical recommendation from a doctor licensed in the state. This is usually done by going to a medical marijuana evaluation center which are opening everywhere. They will have a relationship with a doctor(s) who will provide the recommendation. Qualifying ailments include depression, anxiety, multiple sclerosis, HIV, back pain, glaucoma, cancer and more. Patient must provide proof of residency.

For More Info: California Dept. of Public Health - Office of County Health Services Attn: Medical Marijuana Program Unit, MS 5203 P.O. Box 997377 Sacramento, CA 95899-8600 (916) 552-8600

Colorado

420 Law: Ballot Amendment 20 (2000)

Plant Limit: 2 ounces usable, 6 plants [3 mature, 3 immature]

How to Register: Patients must obtain a Medical Marijuana Registry ID card from the Colorado Dept. of Health and the Environment. Application requires a copy of your Colorado driver's license or ID card, a $90 application fee and a certification form completed and signed by a doctor licensed to practice medicine in Colorado confirming a "debilitating medical condition."

For More Info: Medical Marijuana Registry – Colorado Dept. of Health and Environment 4300 Cherry Creek Drive South Denver, CO 80246-1530 (303) 692-2184

Delaware

420 Law: Senate Bill 17 (July 2011)

Plant Limit: Patients 18 and older with certain debilitating medical conditions may possess up to six ounces of marijuana with a doctor's written recommendation. Amendments to the Bill prohibit smoking in privately owned vehicles and require marijuana be dispensed in sealed, tamperproof containers. The law does not allow patients or caregivers to grow marijuana at home but it does allow for state regulated, non-profit distribution of medical marijuana by compassion centers. A registered compassion center may not dispense more than 3 ounces of marijuana to a registered qualifying patient in any fourteen day period. Patients may register with only one compassionate center.

How to Register: pending

For More Info: The Delaware Dept. of Health and Social Services is responsible for authorizing three not-for-profit compassionate centers and establishing a registry program for patients.

Hawaii

420 Law: Senate Bill 862 (2000)

Plant Limit: 3 ounces usable, 7 plants [3 mature, 4 immature]

How to Register: Patients must register with the Dept. of Public Safety. Application requires your Hawaii driver's license or ID card, a non-refundable $25 fee, and a doctor's written certification confirming a "debilitating medical condition." The doctor must register the patient with the Dept. of Public Safety, which will issue a registration certificate.

For More Info: Narcotics Enforcement Division 3375 Koapaka Street, Suite D-100 Honolulu, HI 96819 (808) 837-8474

Maine

420 Law: Ballot Question 2 (1999)

Plant Limit: 1.25 ounces usable, 6 plants [3 mature, 3 immature]

How to Register: Maine offers no official registration process. A patient may possess a usable amount of marijuana for medical use if, at the time of that possession, the person has available an authenticated copy of a medical record or other written documentation from a doctor. The patient must have a "debilitating or chronic medical condition" and the doctor must have a "bona fide doctor-patient relationship with the person."

For More Info: Dept. of Health and Human Services – Division of Licensing and Regulatory -John Thiele, Program Manager, 11 State House Station Augusta, ME 04333 (207) 287-9300

Maryland

420 Law: Senate Bill 502 (2003)

Plant Limit: N/A

How to Register: Maryland allows an affirmative defense in court for medical marijuana patients in possession of less than an ounce of cannabis but offers them no other regulations or formal protections. Beyond a doctor's recommendation, the state has no registration process, no identification card and no list of eligible medical conditions. Some activist organizations do not list MD among their medical marijuana states.

Update: On May 10, 2011 Maryland Governor Martin O'Malley signed SB 308. SB 308 removed criminal penalties for medical marijuana patients who meet the specified conditions but patients are still subject to arrest. The bill provides an affirmative defense for defendants who have been diagnosed with a debilitating medical condition that is "severe and resistant to conventional medicine." The affirmative defense does not apply to defendants who used medical marijuana in public or who were in possession of more than one ounce of marijuana. The bill also created a Work Group to "develop a model program to facilitate patient access to marijuana for medical purposes."

For More Info: N/A

Michigan

420 Law: Proposal 1 (2008)

Plant Limit: 2.5 ounces usable, 12 plants

How to Register: Patients must obtain a registry identification card from the Michigan Dept. of Community Health. Application requires information about the patient and the patient's doctor and a signed document from the doctor stating the patient's "debilitating medical condition."

For More Info: Michigan Medical Marihuana Program (MMMP) Bureau of Professions, Dept. of Community Health 611 W. Ottawa Street Lansing, MI 48933 (517) 373-0395

Montana

420 Law: Initiative 148 (2004)

Plant Limit: 1 ounce usable, 6 plants

How to Register: Patients must register with the Quality Assurance Program of the Dept. of Health and Human Services. Application requires a Montana driver's license or state ID, a written certification from a doctor of the patient's "debilitating medical condition" and a $50 application fee.

For More Info: Medical Marijuana Program – Montana Dept. of Health and Human Services – License Bureau 2401 Colonial Drive, 2nd Floor Helena, MT 59620-2953 (406) 444-2676

Nevada

420 Law: Ballot Question 9 (2000)

Plant Limit: 1 ounce usable, 7 plants [3 mature, 4 immature]

How to Register: Patients must obtain a registry identification card from the Nevada State Health Division. Applicants must include proof that the patient is a resident of Nevada, written documentation from a doctor of the patient's "chronic or debilitating medical condition" and a $50 application fee. Upon approval, there is an additional $150 registration fee.

For More Info: Nevada State Health Division 1000 E. William Street, Suite 209 Carson City, NV 89701 (775) 687-7595

New Mexico

420 Law: Senate Bill 523 (2007)

Plant Limit: 6 ounces usable, 16 plants [4 mature, 12 immature]

How to Register: Patients must obtain a registry identification card from the Dept. of Health. Applicants must include proof of New Mexico residency and written documentation from the patient's doctor of a "debilitating medical condition." There are no fees in place at this time.

For More Info: New Mexico Dept. of Health 1190 St. Francis Drive P.O. Box 26110 Santa Fe, NM 87502-6110 (505) 827-2321

New Jersey

420 Law: S-119 (2010)

Plant Limit: No self-cultivation

How to Register: Regulations are still being finalized. The program will be run by the Dept. of Health and Senior Services (DHHS).

For More Info: www. state.nj.us/health/med_marijuana.shtml

Oregon

420 Law: Ballot Measure 67 (1998)

Plant Limit: 24 ounces usable [6 mature, 18 immature]

How to Register: Patients must register with the Oregon Medical Marijuana Program, part of the State Dept. of Human Services' Public Health Division. Application requires an Oregon driver's license or ID, a written statement from the patient's doctor confirming a "debilitating medical condition" and a $150 fee (or a $50 fee if the patient is part of the Oregon Health Plan).

For More Info: Oregon Dept. of Human Services P.O. Box 14450 Portland, OR 97293-0450 (971) 673-1278

Rhode Island

420 Law: Senate Bill 0710 (2006)

Plant Limit: 2.5 ounces usable, 12 plants

How to Register: Patients must obtain a registry identification card from the Dept. of Health. Application requires a Rhode Island driver's license or ID, written documentation from a doctor of a "debilitating medical condition" and a $75 registration fee. If you have a medical-marijuana registry card from any other state, you may use it with the same and effect as a card issued by the Rhode Island Dept. of Health.

For More Info: Rhode Island Dept. of Health — Office of Health Professions Regulation 3 Capitol Hill, Room 104 Providence, RI 02908-5097 (401) 222-2828

Vermont

420 Law: Senate Bill 76, House Bill 645 (2004)

Plant Limit: 2 ounces usable, 9 plants [2 mature, 7 immature]

How to Register: Patients must register with the Dept. of Public Safety. Application requires a Vermont driver's license or ID, written documentation from a doctor of a "debilitating medical condition" and a $50 registration fee.

For More Info: Marijuana Registry – Dept. of Public Safety 103 South Main Street Waterbury, VT 05671

Washington

420 Law: Initiative 692 (1998)

Plant Limit: 24 ounces usable, 15 plants

How to Register: Washington offers no formal registration process. Legal patients must have a Washington driver's license or ID and a formal statement signed by a doctor licensed in Washington documenting a "terminal or debilitating medical condition."

For More Info: Dept. of Health P.O. Box 47866 Olympia, WA 98504-7866 (360) 236-4768

Washington, D.C.

420 Law: Initiative 59 (2010)

Plant Limit: The maximum amount of medical marijuana that any qualifying patient or caregiver may possess at any moment is two ounces of dried medical marijuana. The Mayor may increase the quantity of dried medical marijuana that may be possessed up to four ounces; and shall decide limits on medical marijuana of a form other than dried.

How to Register: Pending. Although medical marijuana was overwhelmingly approved by Washington D.C. voters in 1998, U.S.

Congress, which has control over the city's budget, indefinitely blocked its implementation at that time. In December 2009, Congress finally passed a D.C. appropriations bill without a ban on I-59, paving the way for a D.C. City Council debate on how to implement the law.

For More Info: The program shall be administered by the Mayor. The Dept. of Health has yet to announce when the program will begin and how it will run.

Sources: Medical Marijuana Magazine and Procon.org

States Considering Medical Marijuana w Pending Legislation (as of Jan 2012)

Illinois

420 Law: HB-0030 (Introduced 2011)

Sponsors: Deputy Majority Leader Lou Lang (D) and Chief Co-Sponsors Rep. Angelo Saviano (R), Rep. Ann Williams (D), Rep. Kenneth Dunkin (D), Rep. Sara Feigenholtz (D) and Rep. Kelly M. Cassidy

Details: Compassionate Use of Medical Cannabis Pilot Program Act will allow state-registered patients diagnosed by a doctor as having a "debilitating medical condition" to cultivate medical marijuana or to obtain it from state-regulated dispensaries. Amendment 1 will repeal the program after three years and prohibit patients from driving for 12 hours after consuming. Amendment 2 will make it illegal for dispensaries to make campaign contributions. Amendment 3 sets a $5,000 non-refundable application fee and a $20,000 certificate fee for dispensaries.

Massachusetts

420 Law: HB-625 & SB-1161 (Introduced 2011)

Sponsors: Rep. Frank I. Smizik (D) & Sen. Stanley Rosenberg (D) respectively

Details: The Massachusetts Medical Marijuana Act will protect patients with debilitating medical conditions as well as their doctors and designated caregivers from arrest and prosecution, criminal and other penalties and property forfeiture if such patients engage in the medical use of marijuana.

New Hampshire

420 Law: HB-442 (Introduced 2011)

Sponsor: Rep. Evalyn Merrick (D)

Details: "The purpose of this act is to protect patients with debilitating medical conditions, as well as their physicians and designated caregivers from arrest and prosecution, criminal and other penalties, and property forfeiture if such patients engage in the medical use of marijuana."

New York

420 Law: SB-S2774 (Introduced 2011)

Sponsor: Senate Health Committee Chair Tom Duane (D)

Details: "Legalizes the possession, manufacture, use, delivery, transfer or administration of marihuana by a certified patient or designated caregiver for a certified medical use;...directs the department of health to monitor such use and promulgate rules and regulations for registry identification cards." Set possession limit of 2.5 ounces.

Ohio

420 Law: HB-214 (Introduced 2011)

Sponsors: Rep. Kenny Yuko (D) and Rep. Robert Hagan (D)

Details: "There is a presumption that a registered qualifying patient or visiting qualifying patient is engaged in the medical use of cannabis if the patient is in possession of a valid registry identification card or valid visiting qualifying patient identification card."

Pennsylvania

420 Law: SB-1003 (Introduced 2011)

Sponsor: Sen. Daylin Leach (D)

Details: The Governor Raymond Shafer Compassionate Use Medical Marijuana Act provides "for medical use of marijuana; and repealing provisions of law that prohibit and penalize marijuana use."

Source: Procon.org

Countries That Allow For Medicinal Use of Marijuana

UNTIED STATES	CANADA	BELGIUM
CZECH REPUBLIC	PORTUGAL	NETHERLANDS
ISRAEL		

Bibliography

1. Allen, John and Jochen Gartz PhD. The Ancient Legacy of Scared Use. 2001. www.serendipity.li/dmt/cult_a.htm. (accessed April 16, 2012)

2. Berdon, Victoria. Egyptian Medical Texts. www.poytner.indiana.edu/sas/lb/codes.htm

3. Herodotus of the Egyptians in *Histories* Book II, 84

4. Drug Library. Marijuana - The First Twelve Thousand Years. www.druglibrary.org?schaffer?hemp/history/first12000/7.htm. (accessed June 7, 2012)

5. Allen, John and Jochen Gartz PhD. The Ancient Legacy of Scared Use. 2001. www.serendipity.li/dmt/cult_a.htm. (accessed April 16,

6. Wikipedia. Religious and Spiritual Use of Cannabis. www.en.wikipedia.org/wiki/Religious_and_spiritual_use_of_cannabis. (accessed Jan. 10, 2012)

7. Marijuana & the Bible. www.ebeneezer.net/ritual/vegetable/offsite/bible.htm. (accessed Jan. 5, 2012)

8. The Farmers' Register, III (1836), 612

9. Vantreese, Valerie, Thomas D. Clark, University of Kentucky. The Trade between Kentucky and the Cotton Kingdom in Livestock, Hemp, and Slaves. M.A. thesis. 1929. www.utpress.org?Appalachia/EntryDisplay.php?EntryID=015

10. Hopkins, James F. A History of the Hemp Industry in Kentucky. 1998 www.ebeneezer.net/ritual/vegetable/offsite/bible.htm. (accessed Jan. 5, 2012)

11. Weir, Ian. Henry Ford.
www.patriotsplant.com/Henry_Fords_Hemp_Car.html (accessed Dec. 10, 2011)

12. Versitiva Hemp Chronicles. 10 Hemp Facts You Don't Know. May 28, 2011. www.versitivahempchronicles.blogspot.com/2011/05/10-hemp-facts-you-dont-know.html. (accessed Oct. 11, 2011)

13. Procon.org. Top 10 Pros and Cons. May 9, 2009. www.procon.org. (accessed Jan. 1, 2012)

14. Ukcia. Pot Culture 1 1914 - 1937 Reefer Madness. www.ukcia.org (accessed Dec. 22, 2011)

15. U.S. Patent and Trademark Office. Guidelines for Examination of Applications for Compliance With the Utility Requirement. Dec. 27, 2011 www.uspto.gov (accessed Jan. 15, 2012)

16. History of DEA: 1970-1975. DEA Museum.
www.deamuseum.org/dea_history_book/1970_1975.htm (accessed Feb. 2, 2012)

17. Podesta, John. Too Much Secrecy Puts Our Nation at Risk. Sept. 16, 2008. www.americanprogress.org/issues/2008/09/podesta_law_testimony (accessed Feb. 2, 2012)

18. Riog-Franzia, Manuel. Hemp fans look toward Lyster Dewey's past, and the Pentagon, for higher ground. May 13, 2010. www.washingtonpost.com (accessed June 21, 2012)

19. Sircus, Mark. Hemp Oil and Cancer. Feb. 23, 2008. www.thenhf.com/article.php?497

20. Office of National Drug Control Policy. Marijuana. www.whitehouse.gov/ondcp/marijuana (accessed March 7, 2012)

21. Rhodes, Richard. The History of Cannabis Prohibition 1937-1962. www.420magazine.com/forums/cannabis-facts-information/837. (accessed Dec. 9, 2011)

22. Benet, Sula Dr. Early Diffusion and Folk Uses of Hemp. (Reprinted in Cannabis and Culture, Vera Rubin, Ed. pg. 41 The Hague: Mouton, 1975)

23. Kentucky: Lincoln Bicentennial - Emancipation Proclamation. Oct. 3, 2007. www.kylincoln.org/lincoln/africanamerican/emancipation.htm (accessed March 5, 2012)

24. Jaslow, Ryan. Miracle-Gro and Montel Williams want in on marijuana business. June 15, 2011. www.cbsnews.com/8301-504763_162-20071285-10391704.html (accessed March 1, 2012)

25. Wilkerson, Brian. Rep. Henderson, Commissioner Comer stand in support of industrial hemp bill. Press Release. Jan. 9, 2012

26. Idrasil. www.doobos.com/Idrasil_info. (accessed June 7, 2012)

27. Lata, H. et al. Univ. of Mississippi. School of Pharmacy. Assessment of the Genetic Stability of Micro-propagated Plants of Cannabis sativa by ISSR Markers. Planta Med 2010: 76: 97-100

28. Conrad, Chris. Hemp: Lifeline to the Future. 1994. pp. 192-193, part of Chapter 16, "A World of Cannabis Cultures. Creative Xpressions Publications.

29. Burke, Richard. June 21, 1975. Pots & Presidents

30. World Health Organization. Cannabis. www.who.int/substance_abuse/facts/cannabis/en/ (accessed March 8, 2012)

31. Joy, Janet E. et al. and Institute of Medicine. Marijuana and Medicine: Assessing the Science Base. 1999. National Academy Press

32. Lyster Dewey: Hemp 1913 USDA Yearbook of Ag.
www.naihc.org/hemp_information/content/1913.html

33. Digital Egypt for Universities. University College of London website. Knowledge and production: the House of Life.
www.digitalegypt.ucl.ac.uk. (retrieved on Nov. 18, 2011)

34. Nunn, John Francis. Ancient Egyptian Medicine. University of Oklahoma Press. 1999

35. Dvorak, John. Hemphasis: America's Harried Hemp History. 2004.
www.hemphasis.net/History/harriedhemp.htm (accessed Jan. 5, 2012)

36. Austin, Gregory A. Perspectives on the History of Psychoactive Substance Abuse. 1999. The Ibogaine Dossier.
www.ibogaine.desk.nl/drugmain.html. (accessed Dec. 21, 2011)

37. Procon.org. 6 States with Pending Legislation to Legalize Medical Marijuana. August 4, 2011. www.procon.org. (accessed Dec. 31, 2011)

38. Wikipedia. Compassionate Investigational New Drug Program. August, 15 2011.
www.wikipedia.org/wiki/Compassionate_Investigational_New_Drug_Program. (accessed Dec. 21, 2011)

39. New York Times March 14, 1926

40. Cannabis Religions Goddess Plan Pr Ntr Kmt.
www.prntrkmt.org/cannabis/cannabisreligion.html. (accessed June 7, 2012)

41. Procon.org. 16 Legal Medical Marijuana States and DC. Dec. 23, 2011. www.procon.org. (accessed Dec. 31, 2011)

42. Newport, Frank. Record-High 50% of Americans Favor Legalizing Marijuana Use. Oct. 17, 2011. www.gallup.com/poll/150149. (accessed April 16, 2012)

43. Temple M.D., Robert J. Availability of Investigational Drugs for Compassionate Use. June 20, 2011. www.fda.gov/NewsEvents/Testimony?ucm115209.htm. (accessed Dec. 20, 2011)

44. Burke, Richard. Pot & Presidents. June 1975

45. Frazier, Jack. The Great American Hemp Industry.

46. Yurchey, Doug. The Marijuana Conspiracy. www.world-mysteries.com/marijuana!.htm. (accessed Dec. 10, 2011)

47. Kaufman, Mark. Study Finds No Cancer-Marijuana Connection. Washington Post. May 26, 2006

48. Wikipedia. Medical Cannabis. www.en.wikipedia.org/wiki/Medicinal_cannabis. (accessed Dec. 15, 2011)

49. Wikipedia. Legal history of cannabis in the United States. www.en.wikipedia.org/wiki/Legal_history_of_cannabis_in_the_United_States. (accessed Dec. 6, 2011)

50. eHow. Hemp Oil Uses. www.ehow.com/info_8173239_hemp-oil-uses.html. (accessed March 1, 2012)

51. Digital Journal. Cannabis Effective for Easing MS Symptoms, but Not for Slowing Progression. June 2, 2012 www.digitaljournal.com/pr/737012 (accessed June 7, 2012)

52. Antique Cannabis Book. Pot Shrinks Tumors. www.antiquecannabisbook.com/chap1B/Censorship.htm. (accessed Dec. 6, 2011)

53. Reuters. Could smoking pot cut risk of head, neck cancer? www.reuters.com.

54. Office of National Drug Control Policy. Myth 5: Marijuana is used to treat cancer and other diseases. (from booklet Marijuana Myths & Facts: The Truth Behind 10 Popular Misperceptions. www.ncjrs.gov/ondcppubs/publications/pdf/marijuana_myths_facts.pdf.

55. Hemp Sisters. Hemp History. www.hemp-sister.com/Information/history.htm. (accessed Jan. 1, 2012)

www.ingramcontent.com/pod-product-compliance
Lightning Source LLC
Chambersburg PA
CBHW071225290326
41931CB00037B/1973